DISCOVERING
the BASIC TRUTHS
of CHRISTIANITY

DISCOVERING
the BASIC TRUTHS
of CHRISTIANITY

Larry Kreider

DESTINY IMAGE® PUBLISHERS, INC.
P.O. Box 310, Shippensburg, PA 17257-0310

"Speaking to the Purposes of God for this Generation and for the Generations to Come."

This book and all other Destiny Image, Revival Press, Mercy Place, Fresh Bread, Destiny Image Fiction, and Treasure House books are available at Christian bookstores and distributors worldwide.

For a U.S. bookstore nearest you, call **1-800-722-6774**.

For more information on foreign distributors, call **717-532-3040**.

Or reach us on the Internet: **www.destinyimage.com**.

ISBN 10: 0-7684-2748-7

ISBN 13: 978-0-7684-2748-6

For Worldwide Distribution, Printed in the U.S.A.

1 2 3 4 5 6 7 8 9 10 11 / 13 12 11 10 09

DEDICATION

I dedicate this book to my wife LaVerne, to my family, and to the DCFI family worldwide, with whom we have had the privilege of serving the Lord for nearly 30 years. This book is also dedicated to every person who reads this book seeking to lay a strong spiritual foundation in his or her life. And most importantly of all, this book is dedicated to the One who has promised us that He will build His life in us...our Lord Jesus Christ, to whom I am eternally grateful.

For no other foundation can anyone lay than that which is laid, which is Jesus Christ (1 Corinthians 3:11 NKJV).

ACKNOWLEDGMENTS

A very special thanks to my editor and writing assistant, Karen Ruiz, who does a superb job. Also, thanks to the thousands of believers in the DCFI family worldwide who have walked with us as we learned these foundational biblical truths during nearly three decades of serving together. We have been on a journey as we continue to learn to live out these basic truths from the Word of God. Thanks to the numerous spiritual leaders in the Body of Christ at large, from many different denominations, who have offered countless spiritual insights that have helped to shape this book. And a very grateful "thank you" to the DCFI team of leaders, who I have been honored to serve with for more than 25 years and who have labored tirelessly to give me the time to write this book. It is a joy to serve our Lord together with you!

ENDORSEMENTS

Larry Kreider's passion for the Church that Jesus is building is multi-dimensioned. Clearly, as this book indicates, besides being an igniter of evangelism and an initiator of church planting, Pastor Kreider is a leader who instills life-transforming truth in new believers, establishing true disciples for the ongoing growth of God's Kingdom, while resourcing the healthy development of the growing Christian's life and witness.

—Dr. Jack W. Hayford
President, International Foursquare Churches
Chancellor, The King's College and Seminary Founding
Pastor, The Church on the Way

Too often in our churches we neglect the basics. That's why we seem to have such a large number of born-again believers who are dysfunctional. I am elated that Larry Kreider is forcefully bringing us back to the basics in *Discovering the Basic Truths of Christianity* and its sequel, *Building Your Life on the Basic Truths of Christianity*. These two books will cause you to understand what you really believe and how it works out in real life. Larry has provided a wonderful new treasure for the Body of Christ!

—C. Peter Wagner, Chancellor
Wagner Leadership Institute

TABLE OF CONTENTS

INTRODUCTION

In the city of Pisa, workers laid the first stone for a magnificent bell tower. The building materials and workmanship were second to none in the Renaissance era. Yet it soon became clear that something was terribly wrong: a slight "lean" was visible.

The building's brilliant design was already becoming less important than its flawed foundation. Unfortunately, the tower was built on marshy soil only three meters above sea level. Today, the celebrated "Leaning Tower of Pisa" has a reputation as an oddity in architecture.

In nearly 40 years of ministry as a youth worker, pastor, and servant leader, I have watched this same scenario play out in the lives of new Christians around the world. Many launch out in their newly found faith in Jesus Christ with great zeal but start to sink when they are hit with discouragement and problems. In some cases, we see young Christians (and those old enough to know better) erect faulty towers, using the building blocks of their personal abilities, gifts, and vision. Unfortunately, their foundation is as unstable as the marshy soil underneath the Tower of Pisa! Without exception, every one of them desperately needs a solid, biblical foundation for their new lives.

The foundation of the Christian faith is built on Jesus Christ and His Word to us, the Holy Bible. This two-book series of *Biblical*

Foundations includes the foundation of biblical doctrines that you need to help you lay a strong spiritual foundation in your life.

In this first Biblical Foundation book, *Discovering the Basic Truths of Christianity,* we build on the foundation of Jesus Christ, the grace and freedom He gives to us, and the foundational truths found in Hebrews chapter 6:1-2.

These truths from the Word of God are presented with modern-day stories that will help you easily understand the basics of Christianity. Use this book and the second book in this series to lay a solid foundation in your life; if you are already a mature Christian, these two books are great tools to assist you in mentoring others. May His Word become life to you today.

God bless you!

PART I

Knowing Jesus Christ as Lord

Chapter 1

HOW TO BUILD A SOLID FOUNDATION

PERSONAL ENCOUNTER WITH JESUS

Years ago, I worked on a construction crew. I learned quickly that the first step to building a house is to *put in a solid foundation*. Likewise, our Christian lives must be built on the sure foundation of Jesus Christ. He is the foundation for the Christian faith: *"For no one can lay any foundation other than the one already laid, which is Jesus Christ"* (1 Cor. 3:11). If we build on anything else, our spiritual foundation is faulty and will collapse when tests and storms come our way—and we can be sure they will come. If our foundation is strong, we will be able to stand, no matter how hard the winds blow.

This book, and the next in this series, will help you continue to build, once you lay the foundation of a personal encounter with Christ, who claims, *"I am the way and the truth and the life. No one comes to the Father except through Me"* (John 14:6).

Many people have a false understanding of what it means to be *Christian*. Some people think that if you live in a "Christian nation," such as the United States, you are a Christian. Others think they are Christians because their parents are Christians. Being a follower of Jesus is not based on our ethnic or family background. It is based on a relationship. Knowing *about* God does not mean that you know Him personally. You may know about the Queen of England, but you probably do not know her personally. You cannot know God without having a relationship with Him. Christianity is all about having a relationship with the living God.

Liz was attracted to Christianity when a neighbor moved in next door. She recalls, "Judy talked about God in intimate terms, and I could tell she really knew Him. She acted like God lived in the house with her." Liz longed for that same relationship with God, so she, too, yielded her life to Christ.

The basic foundations for a Christian's life must be built on Jesus Christ who wants to know us personally. In this book, we will come to know that God is revealed to us through Jesus Christ:

Now this is eternal life: that they may know You, the only true God, and Jesus Christ, whom You have sent (John 17:3).

GOD WANTS TO KNOW US PERSONALLY

Our universe and everything in it has order and design. Its complexity and beauty suggest an intelligent creator. God intended for the beauty of the universe to point to Him (see Ps. 19:1). In Romans 1:20, the apostle Paul tells us that God has made Himself known to us through nature and an inner, instinctive recognition of God:

For since the creation of the world God's invisible qualities—His eternal power and divine nature—have been clearly seen, being understood from what has been made, so that men are without excuse (Romans 1:20).

In nature, we find evidence that He exists, but He really must be accepted by faith:

And without faith it is impossible to please God, because anyone who comes to Him must believe that He exists and that He rewards those who earnestly seek Him (Hebrews 11:6).

If a person does not want to believe in God, he can find a million reasons not to believe. Yet, when you think about it, it really takes more faith not to believe in God than it does to believe in Him. Take a look at a beautiful sunset or watch the power of waves crashing onto the seashore—it's hard not to believe in God, a master designer, who created all of it.

Many people think of God as a distant, impersonal being, presiding over His creation disinterestedly and intervening only when humans beg Him to act on their behalf. Such a view is entirely incorrect.

The Bible reveals a God who seeks humankind because He wants to fellowship with them. God, the Creator of the universe and Ruler over it, who existed before the beginning of time, created humans in His image. God said, *"Let Us make man in Our image, according to Our likeness..."* (Gen. 1:26 NKJV). He wants mankind to reflect His image. The Creator of the universe wants to have a personal friendship and relationship with you! He wants you to know Him, and He wants to be your closest friend.

This is how God showed His love among us: He sent his one and only Son into the world that we might live through Him (1 John 4:9).

JESUS—THE ONLY WAY TO GOD

We were created to share in a close, loving relationship with God and one another. Relationship is central to God. He created us to live in unbroken fellowship with Him. But the first human beings,

Adam and Eve, created without sin and in perfect fellowship with God, rebelled against God in the Garden of Eden. When Satan tempted them to eat the forbidden fruit from the only tree in the Garden that God commanded them to avoid, their sin of disobedience alienated them from God (see Gen. 3:6,14-19).

Did God leave mankind to perish in their sin? No! He loved them and continued to reach out to them. In the Bible, we do not see man seeking after God; we see God reaching after man.

You did not choose me, but I chose you... (John 15:16).

But what possibility does man have to know the eternal God? God is infinite, all powerful, and all wise (see Isa. 40:12-18; 55:8-9). How can we ever relate to such an awesome God? It is possible through Jesus Christ. God took the initiative to reveal Himself in Jesus Christ. He reached out to us through Christ. We can know the Father through knowing Jesus. Jesus Himself said,

> *If you really knew Me, you would know My Father as well...anyone who has seen Me has seen the Father...* (John 14:7,9).

When we see Jesus, we see Father God. We must accept and believe in Jesus Christ in order to know God.

Some people say that there are many ways to God, but the Bible is clear—no one can come to God and go to Heaven except through Jesus Christ (see John 14:6; Acts 4:12). The Bible tells us that not everyone will be saved (see Matt. 25:41-42) and that it really *does* matter what we believe, regardless of how sincere we are (see Acts 17:22-31).

We must believe, by faith, that Jesus is *"the way and the truth and the life,"* because we can only come to God through Jesus Christ (John 14:6).

REALIZE WE'RE LOST IN SIN

In order to be made right in God's eyes, we need to first realize that we are lost:

For all have sinned and fall short of the glory of God (Romans 3:23).

We have all sinned. The word *sin* literally means to miss the mark [of God's perfect will].[1] It would be highly unlikely for a person practicing target shooting to hit the bull's eye every time. Every now and then, he or she will miss. Sin misses the mark of God's perfect will—as revealed in His Word, the Bible—and separates us from God. All of us have disobeyed God. Jesus came to solve the sin problem of mankind. He first convicts us, or makes us aware, of our sin:

He will convict the world of guilt in regard to sin... (John 16:8).

Someone once asked D.L. Moody, an evangelist in the 19th century, how God could reject him if he had only one or two little sins. Moody responded by saying that, if a man is trying to pull himself up on a roof by holding onto a chain, it only takes one weak link to cause him to fall to the ground. The other links may be in perfect condition. It only takes one sin to cause us to spend eternity separated from God.[2] Moody was right. Even one sin separates us from God. God loves us, but He hates sin.

Sin is like cancer. If one of my family members had skin cancer on his arm, every time I would see it, I would hate it. That is how

God feels about sin. He knows that sin will destroy the people that He has created to be in fellowship with Him. God loves us. He does not want to destroy us. But if we stubbornly cling to our sin, we will be destroyed by it.

Once we realize that we have missed the mark, we must believe that Jesus can rescue us from our lost state that condemns us.

Whoever believes in Him is not condemned, but whoever does not believe stands condemned already because he has not believed in the name of God's one and only Son (John 3:18).

REPENT AND BELIEVE

God, in His great mercy and love, could not leave mankind in a state of sinfulness and condemnation. He loved us so much and did not want to see us perish in our sin: "*...not wanting anyone to perish, but everyone to come to repentance*" (2 Pet. 3:9).

It is God's will that we do not die in our sins because our sins demand a terrible penalty—the death penalty. Or, you could say, our sins pay horrible wages—the wages of death, according to Romans 6:23: "*For the wages of sin is death....*"

We earn or deserve what we work for. If we work for sin—living in confusion and disorder outside of God—death is the wage that we receive for our sins (spiritual separation from God for all eternity). But the good news is that God provides a way out. Even though "the wages of sin is death," God offers us the free gift of salvation and eternal life through Jesus Christ: "*...but the gift of God is eternal life in Christ Jesus our Lord*" (Rom. 6:23b).

God sent Jesus to offer us a new Kingdom that He came to set up in our hearts. This happens when we repent of our sins and believe in the truth of His Gospel: *"Jesus went into Galilee, proclaiming the good news of God. 'The time has come,' He said. 'The kingdom of God is near. Repent and believe the good news'"* (Mark 1:14-15).

God's will is for everyone to turn from their sin to Him. He wants everyone to come to a place of true repentance because it is God Himself who *"...commands all people everywhere to repent"* (Acts 17:30).

The word *repentance* means "to change, to turn around, a reversal of decision, [and] to transform."[3] If you are heading in one direction, "to repent" means that you make a decision to turn around and head the other way. If you're driving somewhere and discover that you're going the wrong way, you must turn around and go in the other direction. It means changing your mind and your actions.

A friend of mine was driving in his car one day while listening to a Christian broadcast on his radio. The speaker began to preach: "Someone is driving on the road right now, and you need to turn your life over to God." My friend was convicted. "That's me!" he said. He pulled his car off to the side of the road, weeping as he repented of his sins and made a decision to follow Christ. His life was totally changed from that time on. His decision involved an outward action of turning away from sin and turning to the Father.

A good description of repentance is this:

[Repentance is] resolutely turning from everything we know to be displeasing to God. Not that we make ourselves better before we invite Him in. On the contrary, it is because we cannot forgive or improve ourselves that we need Him to come to us. But we must be willing for Him to do whatever rearranging He likes when He comes in. There can be no resistance, and no attempt to negotiate on our own terms, but rather an unconditional surrender to the lordship of Christ.[4]

CONFESS JESUS AS "LORD"

We come to Christ by confessing and believing that Jesus Christ can save us from a life apart from God. In the same way, a couple professes their commitment to each other on their wedding day in order to begin their marriage relationship, we acknowledge Jesus Christ as our Lord in order to begin our relationship with God.

That if you confess with your mouth, "Jesus is Lord," and believe in your heart that God raised Him from the dead, you will be saved (Romans 10:9).

A friend of mine struggled with knowing if he was a Christian. I told him to take his Bible and read Romans 10:9. He read it over and over, and finally faith rose up in his heart. One day, he announced excitedly, "Now I know I am really a Christian!" Why did he now know? He was no longer basing his belief on his feelings, but on what God said in His Word. He confessed with his mouth that Jesus is Lord and experienced true salvation.

What does it mean to know Jesus Christ as the Lord of our lives? *Lord* can mean "ruler, king, boss, one in complete control of our lives." Yet it is more than that. Confessing Him as Lord is also a confession of Christ's deity. When we confess Jesus as the Lord of our lives, we are not only confessing that He is in total control of our lives, but that He is God.

When Jesus walked on the earth, Caesar, the ruler, demanded that his subjects make a confession that "Caesar is Lord." The early

Christians refused to make this confession that Caesar was the ultimate authority whom they obeyed. They insisted that "Jesus is Lord." And so many were thrown to the lions or lit on fire to serve as human torches to light the evening parties in Caesar's gardens. The early Christians, who lived during the writing of the New Testament, clearly understood Lordship! It required a total commitment on their part.

In the Bible, the word *Savior* is mentioned 37 times. The word *Lord* is mentioned 7,736 times. In the New Testament, *Savior* is found 24 times and *Lord* 717 times.[5] Both are very important, but the emphasis is on Jesus as the *Lord* of our lives.

Today we have the privilege of confessing Jesus as Lord because we choose to, not because we have to. But on the judgment day, when Jesus returns, everyone will acknowledge His Lordship and kneel before Him, according to Philippians 2:10-11:

That at the name of Jesus every knee should bow, in heaven and on earth and under the earth, and every tongue confess that Jesus Christ is Lord, to the glory of God the Father.

RECEIVE SALVATION

Jesus took your place on the cross two thousand years ago so that you can know God.

For Christ died for sins once for all, the righteous for the unrighteous, to bring you to God... (1 Peter 3:18).

When you receive Him as your Lord, He makes you His child: *"Yet to all who received Him, to those who believed in His name, He gave the right to become children of God"* (John 1:12). One time, while speaking to a group of teenagers in Scotland, I took some money out of my pocket and offered it to a young man in the audience. I told him that he could say, "I *believe* in the money," but that he needed to *receive* the money for it to be his. I said, "If you receive it, it is a free gift from me. You didn't do anything to earn it, but it is yours." Of course, he took it!

You can believe in Jesus, but you only have salvation if you receive God's gift to you—Jesus Christ. Salvation is a free gift; you cannot earn it. You do not deserve salvation, but God gives it to you anyway because He loves you. You have salvation and eternal life if you accept God's gift to you and invite Jesus to be the Lord of your life.

Have you asked Jesus Christ into your life as your Lord and King? If not, you can do it right now. The Scriptures tell us that now is the day of salvation (see 2 Cor. 6:2).

Take a moment and pray the following prayer of salvation. Start your new life in Christ today! Find someone to talk to who can encourage you and help you grow spiritually. Expect the Lord to use you in mighty ways as you get to know Him and respond to His voice. God bless you!

PRAYER FOR SALVATION:

I confess Jesus Christ as the Lord and King of my life. I believe in my heart that He is alive from the dead. Lord, I confess to You that many times I have "missed the mark" and gone my own way. But from this moment on, I receive Jesus Christ as the sacrifice for my sins, and I am a new creation in Jesus Christ. Old things have passed away, and all things have become new. Christ lives in me!

As I have confessed Jesus Christ as my Lord, and I believe in my heart that He is alive from the dead, I know that I am saved! I have received eternal life as a free gift from You! Amen.

ENDNOTES

1. *The New Testament Greek Lexicon,* s.v. "Hamartia," http://www.studylight.org/lex/grk/view.cgi?number=266 (accessed 23 Sept 2008).

2. D.L. Moody, "Where Art Thou" (sermon), http://www.scrollpublishing.com/store/DL-Moody.html (accessed 17 Sept 2008).

3. Derek Prince, *The Spirit-Filled Believer's Handbook* (Lake Mary, FL: Creation House, 1993), 101.

4. John R.W. Stott, *Basic Christianity* (Downers Grove, IL: InterVarsity Press, 1971), 125.

5. Paul R. McReynolds, *Word Study Greek-English New Testament* (Carol Stream, IL: Tyndale House Publishers, 1999); see also http://www.studylight.org/lex/.

BUILDING A SOLID FOUNDATION
REFLECTION QUESTIONS

1. How is it possible to know all about God but to not really know Him? According to John 14:6, how can you know God?

2. What evidence have you seen in your experience or observation that convinces you that humanity is lost?

3. What does having Jesus as the Lord of your life mean to you personally?

4. What is the difference between believing in and receiving Christ? Salvation is a free gift—do you want to receive God's gift of Jesus Christ?

Chapter 2

WE MUST COUNT THE COST

TOTAL COMMITMENT REQUIRED

When I was involved in youth ministry, years ago, I used to tell the young people, "If you want friends, peace of mind, and things to work out in your life, come to Jesus. He will help you." Many of the youth made a commitment to Jesus, but two months later, they were back doing their own thing instead of obeying the Lord. In many cases, they were worse off than before they made a commitment to Christ. They didn't understand that Jesus must be their Lord. They "came to Jesus" for what they could get, rather than receiving Jesus Christ as Lord—the complete ruler of their lives.

The Bible tells us in Romans 10:13 that *everyone who calls on the name of the Lord will be saved.* Calling on the Lord means that we are willing to make Him the master, boss, and ruler of every part of our lives, every minute of the day. It requires a total commitment.

Many times Christians preach a "weak" Jesus. I was guilty. I changed my approach and saw lasting fruit. I told the next group of young people, "Jesus must be Lord over everything in your life. Are you willing to die for Jesus if you have to?" I was amazed at their response. They seriously counted the cost before they made a commitment to Christ, just as Jesus requires, according to Luke 14:33,

"...*any of you who does not give up everything he has cannot be My disciple.*" As a result, they experienced lasting change.

Someone once asked a Christian statesman from Switzerland: "What if you were talking to a young person interested in God, and you told him he must give up everything to follow Christ, but he was not ready? Then he walks away and is hit by a car and is killed. How would you feel about your 'hard line' then?" The elderly Swiss gentleman said, "I would sit down and cry, then I'd pick myself up and go tell the next person the same thing." He knew that a total commitment would be a lasting commitment. He had to tell the truth and allow individuals to make up their own minds.

Jesus requires total commitment. True Christians have Christ as the Lord of every area of their lives, and it will show. To make this kind of commitment, we need to seriously count the cost.

FIRST CONSIDER THE COST

Large crowds were following Jesus. They were excited about following this new leader who spoke with such authority. But Jesus knew that their attachment to Him was mostly superficial. He wanted them to really think about what it meant to follow Him, so He spoke to them in a parable:

Suppose one of you wants to build a tower. Will he not first sit down and estimate the cost to see if he has enough money to complete it? For if he lays the foundation and is not able to finish it, everyone who sees it will ridicule him... (Luke 14:28-29).

Jesus spoke a very clear message concerning the cost of following Him. He stressed that an individual should understand the terms of discipleship and not take it lightly: "*If anyone comes to Me and does not hate his father and mother, his wife and children, his brothers and sisters—yes, even his own life—he cannot be My disciple*" (Luke 14:26). The difference between our love for God and our love for even our dearest family members is as great as the difference between love and hate. We are commanded to love our neighbors as ourselves (see Luke 10:27). Yet when we compare that love to the love we have for God, there is no comparison. If Jesus is the Lord of my life, then He is Lord of my marriage, my money, my family, my possessions, my future; He is Lord of everything!

Years ago, we led a Jewish friend to faith in Christ. As a result, her family and many of her friends rejected her and refused to talk to her. She clearly understood the cost of her commitment in making Jesus the Lord and ruler of her life.

Charles Finney, who lived about 200 years ago, was an evangelist who often preached to students on college campuses. After his death, a survey was taken which revealed that 80 percent of those who had made a commitment to Jesus at those campus crusades were living for God and victorious in their Christian lives several years later.[1] Today, statistics consistently show an 84 to 97 percent fall-away rate, a few years later, of those who give their lives to Jesus at an evangelistic crusade.[2] Finney would preach to students and then tell them to go to lunch and come back later if they really wanted to repent and get right with God. He wanted them to count the cost and make sure that they knew what they were doing. When they *did* repent, they were seriously considering the cost of their commitment to Jesus rather than making a flippant, emotional decision.

DENY YOURSELF, TAKE UP THE CROSS

What does it mean to be totally committed to Jesus? There is an old story about a chicken and a pig walking down the road and passing some hungry-looking men. The chicken said to the pig, "Why don't we give them a breakfast of eggs and ham?"

"That's easy for you to say," replied the pig. "For you, that's only a sacrifice, but for me it's total commitment." The pig would have to die to feed those men.

Christians must literally die to their own desires when they commit their lives to Jesus. Jesus said that we must bear a cross or we cannot be His disciples.

And anyone who does not carry his cross and follow Me cannot be My disciple...any of you who does not give up everything he has cannot be My disciple (Luke 14:27,33).

Publicly carrying a cross in biblical days was the brand of a criminal doomed for execution. Everyone knew that he was going to die. The cost of becoming a follower of Christ is a complete renunciation of all claims to one's own life. Bearing a cross is symbolic of dying to self. Luke 9:23-24 says that we must "take up our cross" daily and follow Jesus:

Then He said to them all, "If anyone would come after Me, he must deny himself and take up his cross daily and follow Me. For whoever wants to save his life will lose it, but whoever loses his life for Me will save it" (Luke 9:23-24).

When you die to your sins, you save your life! You are set free from slavery to sin and become engaged in the service of God, according to Romans 6:22:

But now that you have been set free from sin and have become slaves to God, the benefit you reap leads to holiness, and the result is eternal life.

A young lady in Philadelphia was enslaved in prostitution and drug abuse for years. When she surrendered her life to Jesus, she started wearing a cross-shaped earring to remind herself that she is now a bond slave to Jesus. She is no longer in slavery to sin, but she has chosen to take up the cross and follow Jesus.

Salvation is a free gift from God, but when we receive this free gift, we have a responsibility to serve the living God and to hold nothing back.

JESUS—LORD OF EVERYTHING

Suppose I offer to sell you my car but mention that I want to keep the glove compartment. You'd say, "That's ridiculous! The glove compartment is part of the car. If you sell me the car, it belongs to me—all of it." That's how some people think they can come to Jesus. They say, "Jesus, I give you my life—all but this one thing. (It may be their finances, their future, their thought life, or some sinful habit.)

A rich, young ruler asked Jesus what he must do to inherit eternal life (see Matt.19:16-22). Jesus knew the one area that the man clung to was his riches, so He told him to sell his possessions and give them to the poor. The young man went away sorrowful because his riches meant more to him than the opportunity to walk with Jesus. His riches took first place in his life. Jesus did not give him an easy way out with an installment plan of 25 percent down and easy monthly payments! No, Jesus knew that this young man's god was *money* and that he would have to let it go and allow Jesus to take the place of riches in his heart. *Either Jesus is Lord of all, or He's not Lord at all.*

When you put a puzzle together and one piece is missing, it's so frustrating! Why? It's never complete. There is no fulfillment. Sin frustrates people. Something is missing in their lives; they have no peace. But when Jesus becomes the Lord of their lives, they have a reason to live. He comes to give abundant life, filled with purpose and meaning (see John 10:10). The Bible says,

> *And this is the testimony: God has given us eternal life, and this life is in His Son. He who has the Son has life; he who does not have the Son of God does not have life* (1 John 5:11-12).

When we receive Jesus as our Lord, we begin to experience His life. The Lord wants us to be excited about living!

God has an awesome plan for your life today. But you will never walk in the fullness of what the Lord has in store for you unless you give your entire being to the Lord!

SELL OUT

Jesus expects us to sell out completely to His Lordship because He gave up everything to seek and save us. We see this amazing concept in a story that Jesus told in Matthew 13:45-46, called the Parable of the Pearl.

> *Again, the kingdom of heaven is like a merchant looking for fine pearls. When he found one of great value, he went away and sold everything he had and bought it.*

The merchant (Christ) came seeking men and women (pearls) who would respond to Him and His message of salvation. Jesus gave His life (gave all that He had) to purchase one pearl of great value.

Each Christian is that "one pearl" bought at a great price (see 1 Cor. 6:20).

We can also look at the Parable of the Pearl and see that, because Jesus gave everything to save us, He expects us to sell out completely to Him once we find Him. Individuals who seek for God and find Him (the Pearl of great value) should be willing to sacrifice all other things for Him.

The early Christian disciples knew what it meant to give up everything for Jesus. When Jesus said to fisherman, James and John, "Follow Me," they left their boats and nets—their business, their livelihood—and followed Him. As Matthew sat in his tax collecting station, Jesus came by and said, "Follow Me." Matthew left his position and job, and followed Jesus. Zacchaeus, a wealthy tax collector, climbed a tree to catch a glimpse of Jesus as He passed by. Jesus stopped, looked up at him, and told him that He was coming to his house that day.

Zacchaeus didn't hesitate. He climbed down, took Jesus to his home, and declared he would pay back those whom he had cheated.

Jesus told him, *"Today salvation has come to this house"* (Luke 19:9). Jesus is calling us today. Jesus wants to live His life through us. Let's respond to Him today like Zacchaeus and give it all to Jesus.

IT ALL BELONGS TO HIM

Jesus said that if we are attracted to earthly things, our heart will be enslaved to those things:

For where your treasure is, there your heart will be also (Luke 12:34).

Selling out to Jesus means our interests change from selfish ones to Jesus Christ. Earthly treasure no longer holds us in its grip because we are no longer enslaved to it. We have to surrender all in this world that prevents us from putting God first. This includes every material, physical, and emotional attachment that we have to this world. We have to give God our wallets, savings, homes, families, jobs, hopes, pleasures, past, present, future—everything!

What happens then? When we are willing to lay it all down, we discover that God entrusts it back to us. He says, "I'll give you back your home and family and money, but whenever I want them, you must give them to Me. They are Mine. They all belong to Me." That is what it means to give everything to Jesus. We then realize that we are managers of these things instead of owners. He is the owner!

My family belongs to Jesus. My bank account belongs to Jesus. My house belongs to Jesus. My car belongs to Jesus. Sometimes I stop to pick up a hitchhiker because my car belongs to Jesus, and I believe He wants me to help people in need.

Juan Carlos Ortiz tells the story of people in Argentina who became Christians and sold their homes, cars, and other possessions and gave them to the church. The church gave them back and said, "These all belong to Jesus, use them to serve Him. When someone needs a house to stay in or a ride in a car, we will contact you."[3] That's just how God wants it!

HOW TO BE SPIRITUALLY REBORN

When we trust Jesus, we believe in Him and have a personal relationship with Him as Lord. We allow Him to change us from the inside out. We must trust Him to change us.

One day, an influential religious leader, Nicodemus, secretly met with Jesus in the night and told Him that he was convinced that He was the Messiah. Nicodemus was a good Pharisee who believed that the Messiah would come to set up a political kingdom to free the Jews from Roman domination, and he believed Jesus would accomplish it. Jesus caught the man by surprise when He answered, "...*I tell you the truth, no one can see the kingdom of God unless he is born again*" (John 3:3).

Nicodemus was not ready to believe that Jesus came to change people's hearts or that they could be reborn spiritually. He could not understand that a second birth is a supernatural, spiritual rebirth of our spirits into the heavenly realm of God's Kingdom.

Indeed, understanding the rebirth requires faith on our part because it is a miracle of God. You might wonder, "I'm not sure if I'm reborn yet. How do I know?" Well, a newborn baby never says, "I'm not sure if I'm born yet." You are either born, or you're not. In the spiritual sense, either Christ lives in you and you are a new creature, or He does not and you are not yet in the faith (see 2 Cor. 13:5).

If you are born again, start living the new life of Christ who lives in you.

I have been crucified with Christ and I no longer live, but Christ lives in me. The life I live in the body, I live by faith in the Son of God, who loved me and gave Himself for me (Galatians 2:20).

What an amazing statement. Christ actually lives within you when you receive Him into your life! The same Jesus, who walked the face of this earth two thousand years ago, lives within you!

ENDNOTES

1. *Charles Finney Revival Sermons*, http://www.firesofrevival.com/charlesfinney/index.html (accessed 10 Sept 2008).

2. Patrick McIntyre, *The Graham Formula*, (White Harvest Publishing, 2006), 12.

3. Juan Carlos Ortiz, *Disciple*, (Carol Stream, IL: Creation House, 1975), 35.

COUNTING THE COST
REFLECTION QUESTIONS

1. In your experience, how has losing your life for Jesus actually saved it?

2. In what ways do you sometimes try to keep "glove compartments" for yourself?

3. How do you manage, rather than own, earthly things?

4. Why is it so important to be spiritually reborn?

Chapter 3

TOTAL TRUST REQUIRED

BELIEF VS. TRUST

A Christian must be totally committed to the Lord. We can't straddle the fence in the Kingdom of God. God loves us so much that He sent Jesus to die for our sins. God's Word says that we must believe in Him in order to have eternal life.

For God so loved the world that He gave His one and only Son, that whoever believes in Him shall not perish but have eternal life (John 3:16).

What does it mean to believe in Him? Many people today profess to believe in God or that a God exists. But even the demons believe in the existence of God.

You believe that there is one God. Good! Even the demons believe that—and shudder (James 2:19).

To say that you believe is not enough. There is a big difference between mental belief and trust. To truly believe means to totally trust. When my children were little, they used to stand at the top of the steps in our house and say, "Daddy, catch me!" They did not simply believe in my existence—they completely trusted me, and they were confident that I would catch them when they leapt into my arms.

There's a story of a tightrope walker who walked a tightrope across Niagara Falls. He asked the audience if they believed he could push a wheelbarrow across the rope and they said, "Yes!" But when he told them he needed someone to sit in the wheelbarrow, no one volunteered. Their belief did not involve total trust!

You might say, "Well, as long as I am sincere." It's not good enough to be sincere. Some people are sincerely wrong. I have a friend who thought he was traveling on a highway heading west to Harrisburg, Pennsylvania, but he was going in the wrong direction and ended up in Atlantic City, New Jersey, hundreds of miles from his destination. He was very sincere, but he was sincerely wrong.

Others sometimes say, "As long as I have my doctrine right, I'll be OK." Believing in the right doctrine or having a biblical foundation, in itself, will not save us. We must truly trust in Jesus Christ as Lord and enter into a personal love relationship with Him.

BECAUSE HE IS GOD

We trust God for one reason, because He is God. When we believe He is who He says He is, we will love Him with all of our hearts.

Paul, the apostle, revealed his confident trust in Christ when he declared in Second Timothy 1:12, "...*I know whom I have believed, and am convinced that He is able to guard what I have entrusted to Him for that day.*" Paul did not say, "I know *what* I believe"; he said, "I know *whom* I believed." He had a deep and abiding relationship with a person—Jesus Christ.

God does not expect a blind trust in Him. He reveals who He is in Scripture so that, as we get to know who He is, we can more fully trust Him based on knowledge (Scripture). Trust is based on pre-dictability and character. We learn about God's consistency and character through the Scriptures that reveal what God is like and how He has shown His love and commitment to humankind throughout history.

We do not trust in the Lord for His benefits. Although it is true that He *"daily loads us with benefits"* (Ps. 68:19 NKJV), we trust Him because we love Him. A young man complained to me once, "God doesn't work for me. I served God faithfully and was hoping a certain Christian girl would develop a relationship with me, but it didn't work out. I just cannot trust God anymore." Clearly, he was serving God for selfish reasons. He was trying to use God to gain something for himself.

Anything that means more to us than Jesus is an idol in our lives. If a bride discovered before her wedding that her future husband only wanted to marry her because her dad owned a big company and he wanted to get a good job or to "marry into money," how do you think she would feel? It is clear that the groom is distracted from true love by the idol of money. Idols in our lives can be our education, our homes, our image, even our family or friends. The Lord wants our complete love and trust. First John 5:21 says, *"Dear children, keep yourselves from idols."*

We trust Jesus because He laid down His life for us. If we truly love Him, we will obey Him and trust Him completely to guide our lives. When we trust Him, He fills us with joy and peace:

May the God of hope fill you with all joy and peace as you trust in Him, so that you may overflow with hope by the power of the Holy Spirit (Romans 15:13).

41

UNTRUSTWORTHY FEELINGS

During the first few months after I came to Christ, I sometimes felt like I wasn't a Christian. Sometimes I felt close to God, and sometimes He seemed a million miles away. I grew depressed and defeated because I thought my feelings reflected my spiritual condition. Then, a wise counselor encouraged me to turn to First John 5:13 where it says, *"I write these things to you who believe in the name of the Son of God so that you may know that you have eternal life."*

Believing and trusting God's Word to be true caused faith to rise up in my heart. I knew that I had chosen to believe in Jesus Christ as my Lord and Savior. His Word settled it for me because I believed it to be true. I knew that I could not base my relationship with God on my feelings; in fact, I had to realize that sometimes my emotions do not line up with the truth. I am in relationship with God because He says I am. He gives so many promises in His Word that I can trust. God's Word brought a deepening sense of His love for me and caused me to trust Him, regardless of how I felt at the moment.

Our lives are completely changed when we see ourselves and others according to what God says about us and about Himself, not by how we feel. People's misperceptions about themselves are often based on their misperceptions of God. When we know what God's Word says, we will be guided by the Holy Spirit to walk in repentance, faith, and discipline in our new lives.

A new Christian is a new man or woman with a new nature who is being renewed and changed, according to Ephesians 4:22-24:

You were taught, with regard to your former way of life, to put off your old self, which is being corrupted by its deceitful desires; to be made new in the attitude of your minds; and to put on the new self, created to be like God in true righteous-ness and holiness.

INCOMPLETE CHANGE?

Becoming a Christian happens in a moment. When we give our lives to Jesus, we enter into a new life. Because of God's great mercy, He saves us by washing us clean of our sins, "*...not because we were good enough to be saved but because of His kindness and pity—by washing away our sins and giving us the new joy of the indwelling Holy Spirit*" (Titus 3:5 TLB).

Your spirit is washed clean in an instant as the Holy Spirit comes to live within you. This does not mean, however, that you will never sin again. Your old nature continues to battle with your new nature, and you have a part to play so that you can live victoriously.

So I say, live by the Spirit, and you will not gratify the desires of the sinful nature. For the sinful nature desires what is contrary to the Spirit, and the Spirit what is contrary to the sinful nature. They are in conflict with each other, so that you do not do what you want. But if you are led by the Spirit, you are not under law (Galatians 5:16-18).

Sinful desires still may tug at you, but now you also have the Holy Spirit pulling you toward holiness. Your very nature has been changed, and it is your new nature to obey God. The power that sin had in your life is now broken, and a way of victory is provided: the Holy Spirit helps you to overcome sin. As a Christian, it will be impossible for you to live *habitually* in sin because you are born again into a new life. The Lord will bring to mind any unconfessed sin in your life because He is a merciful God.

Suppose I give you a book and three weeks later discover that I still have two pages that belong in that book. I would make sure that you get the pages so that you do not miss any pertinent information. Similarly, the Lord does not want us to miss anything that would keep us from experiencing a Spirit-led Christian life. He will reveal areas of our lives that need cleansing and help us to become victorious in those areas.

A man I know grew up hating a group of neighbors who were of a different nationality. Even after he became a believer, he looked at those people with disdain just because of their nationality. Finally, he read in the Scriptures that everyone is on the same footing in the family of God, regardless of their background (see Rom. 10:12). He broke down and repented for his sin of hatred toward these people. God gave him a new heart toward his neighbors, and he became friends with several of them. If we are open, God will continue to purify us, change us, and give us victory over sin in our lives.

JESUS FORGIVES US COMPLETELY

When Jesus forgives our sins, He forgives them no matter how many we have committed or how bad they were. All our past sin is gone, wiped spotless by His blood shed on the cross.

Blood, in both the Old and New Testaments, stands for death. Christ died, providing a divine substitute for us, as sinners. He became the substitute that would pay the penalty for our sin, permanently! First John 1:7 says that Jesus' shed blood purifies us from sin: "*But if we walk in the light, as He is in the light, we have fellowship with one another, and the blood of Jesus, His Son, purifies us from all sin.*"

When our dirty clothes are washed with detergent, they come out spotless. The blood of Jesus is the most potent detergent in the universe. It completely cleanses us from all sin. This purification is an ongoing work of continual cleansing in the life of every believer. As believers, we make every effort by His grace to walk in the light so that we can have intimate fellowship with God and each other.

A woman once washed Jesus' feet with her tears because she was so grateful for the forgiveness of her sins. Jesus said, "*...her many sins have been forgiven—for she loved much*" (Luke 7:47).

Real love for Jesus comes from a deep awareness of our past sinfulness and His complete forgiveness. Some feel that they have made such terrible mistakes and sinned so horribly that God could never forgive them. Nothing could be further from the truth. No matter what the sin, *everyone* is forgiven for much because God loves to forgive sin when we repent.

SINS ARE NOT REMEMBERED

When we repent of our sins, God forgives us and will never remember or mention them again. Psalm 103:12 tells us that "*as far as the east is from the west, so far has He removed our transgressions from us.*"

You can't get any farther than that! It is as far as you can imagine. When Jesus forgives our sins, He forgets them, period. God gives us a wonderful promise in Micah 7:19. He says that He will "*...tread our sins underfoot and hurl all our iniquities into the depths of the sea.*"

This promise paints an awesome word picture. Our sins sink to the depths of the ocean, never to rise again. God not only casts our sins into the deepest sea, I believe He also puts a sign there that says, "No Fishing!"

When the Egyptians pursued the Israelites into the Red Sea, not one Egyptian was left to pursue God's people. They all perished in the sea. Likewise, no sin that we have confessed can survive God's forgiveness. Like the Egyptians and their chariots, our sins *"...sank like lead in the mighty waters"* (Exod. 15:10). Our sins are totally forgiven, never to be remembered again. The Lord has forgotten our sins as if they have never been, and He wants us to forget them too. We are totally set free when Jesus forgives our sins. We can trust Him.

WE CAN COUNT ON HIM

Our trust in the Lord is a sure hope or confidence that is based on His promises. We can place our confident hope and trust in the Lord, who promises not to disappoint us: *"And hope does not disappoint us, because God has poured out His love into our hearts by the Holy Spirit, whom He has given us"* (Rom. 5:5).

The psalmist puts this trust and hope into perspective in Psalm 146:3-5 when he says,

> *Do not put your trust in princes, in mortal men, who cannot save. When their spirit departs, they return to the ground; on that very day their plans come to nothing. Blessed is he whose help is the God of Jacob, whose hope is in the Lord his God.*

We cannot trust mere mortal men, but we can trust our God! We can count on Him to deliver what He has promised. He gives us hope.

I am blessed when my children believe me when I make a promise to them. It would grieve me if they would not trust me. Our heavenly Father feels the same way about us, His children. He has proved Himself faithful to us. We can totally trust Him and His Word. The basis for our trust in God comes from the very nature of God, of Jesus Christ, and His Word. We cannot place our trust in other human beings or material possessions or money or any other thing on this earth. Our abiding trust can only come from the Lord who *"does not disappoint us"* (Rom. 5:5).

TOTAL TRUST
REFLECTION QUESTIONS

1. What are some idols that you may have in your life?

2. Why are feelings so unreliable?

3. How has God's Word caused faith to rise up in your life?

4. According to First John 1:7, what purifies you from sin? Reflect on how you have experienced God's love and forgiveness of sins.

Chapter 4

HOT, COLD, OR LUKEWARM?

NEITHER HOT NOR COLD?

If we are apathetic about our relationship with Jesus, we are like a glass of lukewarm water, neither hot nor cold. Did anyone ever give you a cupful of warm water on a hot summer day when you wanted a refreshing gulp of cold water? What a letdown! You probably spit it out of your mouth in disappointment! In the same way, Jesus detests lukewarmness in us.

The Laodicean church was filled with lukewarm Christians who compromised with the world. They professed to be Christians, but they resembled the world more than Christ. Christ said that they did not realize it but that they were *"wretched, pitiful, poor, blind and naked"* (Rev. 3:17).

The Lord warns this church about their spiritual condition in Revelation 3:15-16 and tells them that they will be judged:

I know your deeds, that you are neither cold nor hot. I wish you were either one or the other! So, because you are lukewarm—neither hot nor cold—I am about to spit you out of my mouth.

God hates lukewarmness. He wants our full commitment rather than a compromise with the world, resulting in apathy. Our lukewarmness leaves a bad taste in His mouth, and He will vomit us out!

SPIRITUAL COMPROMISE

As we just learned, the Lord wants us to completely commit to Him with no compromise. Lukewarmness is repulsive to Him. We cannot try to have one foot in God's Kingdom and one foot in the kingdom of darkness. This kind of hypocrisy produces spiritual compromise and displeases God.

One reason that God is so concerned about lukewarmness is because He knows that people are watching our lives. The Bible says that our lives are like a letter that God writes to people who are watching us:

> *You yourselves are our letter, written on our hearts, known and read by everybody* (2 Corinthians 3:2).

Our lives are the only Bible that many people ever read. Let's examine our spiritual lives today. Are we lukewarm? If we do not find ourselves hot—excited about the things of God—let's follow the prescription of the Lord. It's found in Revelation 3:19: "*...become enthusiastic about the things of God*" (TLB).

It is our choice. I wake up each morning and make a decision to confess the truth of the Word of God to myself throughout the day. Jesus has come that I might have life. I will experience His abundant life rather than discouragement, confusion, and fear as I daily surrender to Him. I am choosing to be hot! How about you?

A WAY THAT SEEMS RIGHT

There's a story told of a cruise ship with passengers divided into first-class and second-class accommodations. After a few days at sea, the captain announced that, from now on, everyone would be treated first-class, no matter what they paid. There would be lobster and fine cuisine for all. The people were excited, gorged themselves on food, and exclaimed that he was the greatest captain in the world. Only the captain knew the real truth behind his offer—the ship was sinking, and in a short time all would die.

That's the way the devil lies to us. He says, "You can have it all, don't worry—eat, drink, and be merry. You can determine your own truth. God doesn't really require that you live a holy life. Everybody else is doing it." But our own wisdom cannot determine wrong and right. Only God's Word can do that. Only by God's Word can we tell if we are on the right path of life. The devil would prefer that we remain blinded and ignorant because he doesn't want people to know that the Bible says,

There is a way that seems right to a man, but in the end it leads to death (Proverbs 14:12).

In order to determine the right way in life, we must follow God's written revelation in the Bible. Any other path leads us to spiritual death. We cannot allow ourselves to be deceived.

The devil's plan for our lives is to kill us, steal from us, and destroy us. He steals peace, joy, and hope from the lives of those the Lord has created to experience true vibrant life. Jesus Christ came to give us life, abundant life, filled with enthusiasm and joy! Jesus said it like this:

The thief does not come except to steal, and to kill, and to destroy. I have come that they may have life, and that they may have it more abundantly (John 10:10 NKJV).

The Bible tells us that Jesus came to destroy the works of the devil (see 1 John 3:8). It seems foolish not to want to be on God's winning team!

TURNED FROM OUR FIRST LOVE

When we are spiritually lukewarm, we have turned away from our first love for Jesus. A new love is exciting and vibrant. But love loses its luster when communication wanes. If we no longer communicate in a relationship with our heavenly Father, our love for Him will falter. Perhaps you asked Jesus Christ into your life as your Lord a long time ago, but now you have forsaken your first love for Him.

The Ephesian church had a deep love and devotion to Christ at first, but in Revelation 2:4-5, the Lord warned them that their current relationship with Him was lacking. Although they did a lot of good things and worked hard for the Gospel's sake, their heartfelt love for Jesus had died: "...*You have forsaken your first love. Remember the height from which you have fallen! Repent and do the things you did at first....*"

Just because we knew the Lord in a personal way in the past does not necessarily mean that we have a close relationship with Him today. I was making a point of this truth while speaking at a public high school. I asked the students, "Do any of you still know your first grade teacher?" I was startled when a girl in the back of the room raised her hand and said, "Sure I do. She is my mother!" Her point was well taken. The other students, however, had not maintained a relationship with their first grade teacher, so their current relationship with her was nonexistent. Do you have a vital relationship with your heavenly Father today? He is still there, waiting for you to come back to Him:

> *Come near to God and He will come near to you...* (James 4:8).

HE KNOCKS AT YOUR HEART'S DOOR

Maybe you knew Jesus Christ in a personal way in the past, but you are far from Him today. You have forsaken your once vibrant love for Jesus. In Revelation 3:20, Christ speaks an invitation for the lukewarm people at the church of Laodicea to come back into fellowship with Him. He is pictured as standing outside the door, waiting to be invited in once more.

Jesus is also knocking at the door of our lives, waiting for us to repent of our lukewarmness and to open the door to invite Him in. Jesus not only warned the Laodicean church of their condition, He immediately invited them to repent and be restored into fellowship with Him again:

> *...I stand at the door and knock. If anyone hears My voice and opens the door, I will come in and eat with him, and he with Me* (Revelation 3:20).

This invitation is spoken outside the door, as Jesus knocks and asks to be readmitted into their presence. He promises that, if they repent from their lukewarmness and lack of love for Him, He will completely restore them. What an amazing promise! Jesus wants to have a personal relationship with you today. If you have turned away from God, He wants you to again open the door of your life to Him. And when you open the door, He will come in and again fellowship with you.

THE POWER OF YOUR TESTIMONY

After you receive Jesus Christ as the Lord of your life, it is important to give your testimony as often as possible to as many people as possible. One of the ways that you overcome satan is by speaking out for Christ. Revelation 12:11 says,

They overcame him by the blood of the Lamb and by the word of their testimony....

Spiritual power is released when we testify about how the Lord has changed and is changing our lives! Every Christian has an important personal story to tell of how he or she came to know Jesus Christ as Lord. Never be ashamed to speak for Christ:

So do not be ashamed to testify about our Lord, or ashamed of me His prisoner. But join with me in suffering for the gospel, by the power of God, who has saved us and called us to a holy life—not because of anything we have done but because of His own purpose and grace...(2 Timothy 1:8-9).

People will listen when we tell our stories of how we came to believe in Jesus. They will not be intimidated because they are not forced to agree or disagree with the statements we make. It is our story, and they cannot deny how we were persuaded to follow Jesus. When we share our stories, we should focus on the fact that God loves them and that Jesus died for them so that they can be forgiven and made new. We should tell them of the changes that the Lord has made in our lives, which will give them hope for their lives too.

REAL OR COUNTERFEIT?

To some people, Christianity is based on their outward appearance or on what they do rather than a real love for the Lord. They appear righteous outwardly, but inwardly they are not born of God and the Spirit. Jesus sternly reprimanded the Pharisees and scribes in Mark 7:6 for this kind of hypocrisy: *"...These people honor Me with their lips, but their hearts are far from Me."*

For years, I was in the same league as the Pharisees. I considered myself a Christian, but I was living a counterfeit Christian life. Here's my story: my family attended church every Sunday during my childhood. When I was 11 years old, we went to a special evangelistic meeting. I really didn't want to go to hell, so I stood up when the evangelist gave an "altar call." I was later water baptized to become part of the church.

What I really wanted that night was "fire insurance." I decided that Christianity would keep me out of hell, but that was as far as it went. My commitment to the Lord was incomplete, so it wasn't long before I was living a fake Christian life. I only acted like a Christian when I was with my Christian friends. (This is also called hypocrisy.) Seven years later, a friend confronted me: "If you were to die tonight, are you sure you would go to Heaven?" I honestly didn't know the answer, so I said, "Nobody knows that."

The young lady didn't hesitate with her answer. She said, "Well, *I* know."

I had come face to face with the truth. Sure, I could talk about God and the Bible. However, I couldn't talk about *Jesus* because I didn't *know* Him in a personal way. I had made a type of commitment to the Lord, but I believed that somehow God would accept me if I did enough good things along the way. I didn't realize that eternal life comes only through faith in *Jesus Christ as Lord*.

Later that night, when I opened my Bible at home, everything seemed to be written directly to me. I read where Jesus said, "You hypocrites!" and I knew that I was a hypocrite too. My friends considered me to be "the life of the party," but I knew the truth. Loneliness was my companion every evening that I spent at home alone. Even worse, I was afraid that if I died in the night, I would die without God for eternity. I came to the realization that I was living a counterfeit Christian life. That night I said, "Jesus, I give You my life. If You can use this rotten, mixed-up life, I'll serve You the rest of my life."

God miraculously changed me the moment I reached out in faith to Him. My attitudes and desires changed. Even my thinking began to change. This time, I was clearly born again because Jesus Christ had become my *Lord*. I was a new creation in Christ, and I am eternally grateful to Jesus.

If you are trying to appear righteous but continue to pursue sinful directions in your heart and mind, you may be living a counterfeit Christian life. Now is the time to ask the Holy Spirit to shine God's light on your heart. Come to the cross of Jesus, confess your sin, and accept God's forgiveness.

Pray this prayer of confession and repentance and receive God's unconditional love and forgiveness.

Lord, I have been trapped in the web of hypocrisy and long for the freedom that I can have in You. I confess that I have tried to be righteous without You and have been living a counterfeit Christian life. Please forgive my sin so that I can come under the power, control, and influence of Your righteousness.

Thank You for setting me free, Jesus. I pray for courage and wisdom to live out my new life in Christ and experience the fullness and freedom that You desire for me to have.

HOT, COLD, OR LUKEWARM?
REFLECTION QUESTIONS

1. In what ways do you resemble the world more than Christ?

2. How is it possible to have one foot in God's Kingdom and one in the kingdom of darkness? Why is it important for you to become enthusiastic about the things of God?

3. Why is it important for you to give your testimony as often as possible?

4. How are some professing Christians counterfeit? How can you know the difference?

PART II

The New Way of Living

Chapter 5

WORKS vs. FAITH

REPENTANCE FROM DEAD WORKS

After I received Jesus Christ as the Lord of my life, I realized that I had to rebuild my life on a new foundation of the truths found in the Word of God. To grow in my Christian life, I first had to lay down elementary principles of Christianity. Only then could I build upon them to grow in greater maturity.

The spiritual building blocks to build into our lives are basic truths that are found in the Word of God. Starting with this chapter and continuing through Chapter 16, we will examine each of the six spiritual building blocks found in Hebrews 6:1-2:

> *Therefore, leaving the discussion of the elementary principles of Christ, let us go on to perfection, not laying again the foundation of repentance from dead works and of faith toward God, of the doctrine of baptisms, of laying on of hands, of resurrection of the dead, and of eternal judgment* (NKJV).

Here, we are urged to move on to maturity, after building on the elementary principles of 1) repentance from dead works, 2) faith toward God, 3) baptisms, 4) laying on of hands, 5) resurrection of the dead, and 6) eternal judgment. The six principles listed in these verses help us build a solid foundation in our spiritual lives.

Let's look at the first and second foundational stones listed here: "repentance from dead works and faith toward God." We will learn that true repentance always goes before true faith: "...*the foundation of repentance from dead works and of faith toward God*" (Heb. 6:1 NKJV).

"Repenting from dead works" means realizing that all of the good deeds we do will never get us to Heaven. Salvation comes only through faith in the Lord Jesus Christ. People who hope they can "work" their way to Heaven by doing good and avoiding wrong should know that the Bible tells us that

> ...*whoever keeps the whole law and yet stumbles at just one point is guilty of breaking all of it* (James 2:10).

The truth is that no one can keep the law of God because, if we stumble in even one point (and we will because we have a sin nature), we are guilty. In other words, whether I have sinned one time or a million times, I have broken the law. If an airplane crashes 500 feet from the runway or 500 miles from the runway, it still crashes, and the casualties are devastating.

Nothing good that you do will get you to Heaven, but Christ will get you there!

TRUE OR FALSE REPENTANCE?

We already mentioned that repentance means to change our mind and our actions. Repentance is "an inner change of mind resulting in an outward turning around; to face and to move in a completely new direction."[1]

Godly sorrow accompanies true repentance. We find ourselves truly sorry that our sin has grieved the heart of a holy God. This sorrow will produce true repentance, a willingness to change our actions. When we experience true repentance, we can enjoy the forgiveness and the freedom that Jesus gives us.

There is such a thing as *false repentance*, however. False repentance is repenting for any other reason except that God is worthy of our complete obedience. For example, children who are caught doing something wrong by their parents may regret they were caught without ever feeling sorry for disobeying their parents. This is false repentance, which, in reality, is not repentance at all.

How many times have we been guilty of doing the same thing? If we are only sorry that "we got caught" instead of genuinely being sorry for grieving the heart of God, then we have not truly repented. That means that we cannot experience God's forgiveness either. Second Corinthians 7:10 tells us that "*godly sorrow brings repentance that leads to salvation and leaves no regret, but worldly sorrow brings death.*"

The Bible says that Judas, who betrayed Jesus, repented. But he did not experience true repentance. His "repentance" was only remorse and regret. He did not change his mind and direction as biblical repentance requires. In fact, after he felt terrible remorse, he went and hanged himself (see Matt. 27:5). He could no longer find a place of repentance. He could find no way to change his mind.

Just being sorry is not enough. We must trust God to completely change us inside. When we truly repent, Jesus' blood cleanses us from our sin, and we can go on to live a new life in a new way. True repentance means that we realize that we have sinned against a holy God, and our inner change of mind results in a change in our direction.

Although God gives us salvation and forgiveness after true repentance, we may still suffer the consequences of our past sins. Parents may instruct their child not to play on the highway, but if the child disobeys, he could be struck by a car and end up in the hospital. The parent will forgive and help the disobedient child, whom they love, but the child will still experience the pain of his disobedience. Broken relationships and families, loss of trust, sexual diseases, or bad habits are all examples of natural consequences of past sin. But the Lord promises to give us the strength to work through the consequences and to help us live victoriously (see Phil. 4:13).

Sometimes we will also have to pay a price for our past sin. For example, a man guilty of murder who later comes to Christ is forgiven of his sin by God, but he still has to pay a price for the consequences of his actions. His sorrow and repentance will not keep him from serving a prison sentence for his crime.

GOOD WORKS VS. DEAD WORKS

Now that we understand the *repentance* part of *repentance from dead works*, what are "dead works?" Our works refer to good deeds or good things that we do. A dead work is any work, or good deed, that we do to try to earn favor with God. No amount of human goodness, human works, human morality, or religious activity can gain acceptance with God or get anyone into Heaven.

People in certain parts of Malaysia perform a peculiar ritual to appease their gods and try to gain favor with them. Every year they choose one young man from their tribe and sink hooks into the flesh of his back. Then a rope is attached to the hooks in the young man's back, and a cart is loaded with a one-foot-high statue of the local god. The people believe they can gain right standing with their god when the blood-covered young man pulls the idol and cart through their town.

This may sound like a strange and senseless thing for someone to do, yet we are doing a similar thing when we trust in our good works to try to please God. The devil has his hooks in our minds, making us believe that we are accepted by the Lord because of the good things that we do. This is entirely wrong thinking and in opposition to what God's Word says in Ephesians 2:8-9:

> *For it is by grace you have been saved, through faith—and this not from yourselves, it is the gift of God—not by works, so that no one can boast.*

We have been saved through faith. We have favor with God because we have placed our trust in the person and work of Christ. Only Jesus Christ gives us real life. Works are totally incapable of producing spiritual life in us. And yet, we can get caught in the trap of trying to win God's favor by our works. These actions are dead works.

Paul the apostle chided the Galatian Christians because they had started out by faith in Christ, but were now trying, through religious dead works, to gain spirituality:

> *You foolish Galatians! Who has bewitched you? ....Did you receive the Spirit by observing the law, or by believing what you heard? Are you so foolish? After beginning with the Spirit, are you now trying to attain your goal by human effort? ....Does God give you His Spirit and work miracles among you because you observe the law, or because you believe what you heard* (Galatians 3:1-3,5).

Dead works can be very religious. If Christians place their faith in their witnessing, or their Bible reading, or their attendance of church meetings, instead of putting their faith in God, these good deeds become dead works. Being involved in the church, helping the poor, giving offerings, being a good husband or wife or an obedient child—all of these can be dead works if we are trying to gain favor with God through doing them.

I have met people who think that, if they break their bad habits, God will accept them. They say, "I'll stop smoking, and then God will accept me." God does not accept us because we have overcome a bad habit. He accepts us because His Son, Jesus Christ, died on the cross two thousand years ago for our sins, and when we receive Him, we become His sons and daughters. When we give our lives to Jesus, He will give us the power and grace to stop smoking or discontinue any other habit that does not bring glory to God. But He accepts us as we are and gives us the grace and desire to change.

Our goodness does not bring us favor with God. We already have favor with God! God has called us to do good works, but we do them because we already have His favor, not to gain His favor.

WORKS CANNOT SAVE US

So now we know that good works are powerless to help us through the pearly gates of Heaven. The Bible tells us that even the best "good works" that we do to please God are like filthy rags compared to His goodness:

...all our righteous acts are like filthy rags... (Isaiah 64:6).

That is why any good deed done to impress God or man is a "dead work." There's a story that is told about a beggar who was walking down the road one day when he saw the king approaching with his entourage. The beggar was awestruck. Then the king looked down on the beggar and said, "Come, sit on my horse with me." The beggar was astounded. "Why would the king do such a thing?" he wondered.

The beggar laid his questions aside and mounted the king's horse. They rode to the palace together, and as they entered the royal residence, the king said to the beggar, "Today I have chosen you to live in my palace. I'm going to give you new garments to wear and all of the sumptuous food that you can eat. I will make sure that all of your needs are met."

The beggar thought for a moment. All that he had to do was to receive from the king what he had promised to give him. This was too good to be true. He didn't deserve this royal treatment. It just did not make sense. How could the king accept him and meet all of his needs when he had done nothing to deserve it?

From that time on, the beggar lived by the king's provision. However, the beggar thought, "I think I should hang onto my old clothes just in case the king doesn't really mean what he said. I don't want to take any chances." So, the beggar hung onto his old rags...just in case.

When the beggar was old and dying, the king came to his bedside. When the monarch glanced down and saw the old rags still clutched in the beggar's hand, both men began to weep. The beggar finally realized that, even though he had lived his whole life with the king in a royal palace, he had never really trusted the king. Instead, he had chosen to live his entire life under a cruel deception. He should have lived like a royal prince.

Many of us do the same thing. We give our lives to Jesus, but we insist on hanging onto and trusting in our works and the good things we do, "just in case." However, trusting these "dead works," instead of placing our entire confidence in Jesus Christ, is like hanging onto filthy rags from God's perspective. The Lord does not receive us because of our good works. No, we're received by God only because of faith in His Son Jesus Christ and what He has done for us on the cross. We are righteous by faith in Him. Let's not get caught, at the end of our lives, clinging to our old rags, because somehow we found it too hard to believe that the Lord desires to bless us and fill us with His life, even though we do not deserve it at all.

GOD'S PERSPECTIVE ON GOOD WORKS

Should we do good works, then? Yes, absolutely! God wants us to do good works. We show our love by actions. We should do millions of good works in our lifetime, but only because God loves us and has accepted us already; we cannot try to earn His favor. Works play no part at all in securing salvation. But after we reach out to the Lord in faith and know that He accepts us and loves us just the way we are, we will find ourselves wanting to obey God. We will want to do good works because God has changed us. Paul told the Ephesians,

> *For we are God's workmanship, created in Christ Jesus to do good works, which God prepared in advance for us to do* (Ephesians 2:10).

God empowers us to live the Christian life so that we will want to act on the great love He has bestowed on us! I don't take care of my children so that I can be their father; I take care of my children because I am their father and love them deeply. We don't do good works because we want to become righteous; we do good works because we are righteous.

I once read a story about an 8-year-old boy who was instructed by his mother to hoe the family garden. His mother told him to hoe two rows of beans. She showed him exactly how she wanted him to do it and told him, "Now, when you get through, tell me so I can come and look it over." When he finally finished according to her instructions, he called her to inspect it. She took one look at it and shook her head in disapproval, "Well, son, it looks like you're going to have to redo this. For most boys this would be all right. But you are not most boys: you are my son. And my son can do better than this!" Did his mother stop loving him because he did not hoe the garden to perfection? No. She simply expected that he could do better. God's life in us produces good works and changed character. His love for us motivates us to want to reach out to others and to do good works for the right reasons—because we love Him with all our hearts.

TRUE RIGHTEOUSNESS

In Romans 10:2-3, we read about some religious people who had zeal for God but were trying to gain their salvation by their own merits. They tried to establish their own righteousness, or *right standing* with God on their own terms:

> *For I can testify about them that they are zealous for God, but their zeal is not based on knowledge. Since they did not know the righteousness that comes from God and sought to establish their own, they did not submit to God's righteousness.*

These people did not know God's method of saving sinners. They did not realize that they are saved only through faith in Jesus Christ.

Instead, they tried to establish their own righteousness. They were sincere in their efforts, but sincerely wrong.

This reminds me of the young football player who finally caught the ball and took off with a great burst of speed—toward the other team's goal. This young man had zeal, and he ran as fast as he could, but he was headed in the wrong direction! He had misdirected zeal. Our zeal is misdirected if it is not founded on correct views of truth. Our good works cannot obtain favor with the Lord.

Once, when I was in a Latin American country with a friend, we needed to pay with pesos to take our flight out of the country. We didn't have pesos, so we offered them American dollars, which were worth more than the pesos. No matter how hard we tried, they would not accept them. The government had set up their monetary system on pesos, and we were using the wrong system. We had zeal, but our way didn't work.

We must be more than sincere: we must know the truth. We have to yield our hearts to Jesus Christ. Right standing with God only comes through faith in Jesus Christ. Satan will tempt us to trust in something—anything—other than the finished work of Jesus Christ for our salvation. Some people accept Jesus as Lord but add on all kinds of good works with hopes of becoming more righteous. God does not accept us because we eat the right foods, read the Bible in the right way, pray the right way, or dress the right way. Our acceptance is in Jesus, period! We may do some of the above-mentioned good works, but we do not do them in order to be accepted by the Lord. We do them because we *have* been accepted.

A PILE OF RUBBISH

Paul the apostle was of pure Jewish descent, had a prestigious Greek education and was one of the most influential interpreters of Christ's message and teaching as an early Christian missionary. But he considered all the knowledge and the great things he had done as a pile of garbage compared to knowing Jesus Christ. Paul says in Philippians 3:7-8,

But whatever was to my profit I now consider loss for the sake of Christ. What is more, I consider everything a loss compared to the surpassing greatness of knowing Christ Jesus my Lord, for whose sake I have lost all things. I consider them rubbish, that I may gain Christ.

Those who trust in their Christian background, training, or credentials to make them acceptable to God are trusting in the wrong things. If you grew up in a good Christian home and had the opportunity to get Bible training, thank God for it. However, even these good things are rubbish compared to knowing Jesus as Lord and trusting in His righteousness.

Knowing Christ and having an intimate relationship with Him is much more important than what we do or have done for Him. I am thankful that my wife cooks my meals and washes my clothes, but these good works mean nothing compared to our love relationship together. I just enjoy knowing her most of all. The same principle applies to our relationship with Jesus.

If you have trusted your good works or your background more than your relationship with Jesus, you can repent now. Jesus wants to fill you with His love so that you can experience His righteousness and His acceptance.

When we repent, we do an "about face"—we are sharply turned around! If we move from one geographical area to another, we need to change schools or jobs. We go from one to another. True repentance always goes before true faith. So then, in our spiritual lives, we must repent of placing our faith in dead works and do an "about face" by placing our faith in the living God alone!

ENDNOTES

1. Derek Prince, *The Spirit-Filled Believer's Handbook* (Lake Mary, FL: Creation House, 1993), 101.

WORKS VS. FAITH
REFLECTION QUESTIONS

1. What is the difference between true repentance and false repentance? What must be your only reason for repenting?

2. If your good works are not pleasing to God, how do you explain Ephesians 2:10? Why does God expect good works from you? What must be your only motivation for doing good works?

3. How do people try to establish their own righteousness? How can you know that your "zeal for God" does not result in dead works?

4. Is knowing Jesus personally the most important thing in your life?

Chapter 6

FAITH
in GOD

FAITH TOWARD GOD

In the previous chapter, we learned that we must repent from trying to gain God's acceptance by doing good things (see Heb. 6:1). Good deeds done to impress God or man are "dead works," and they do not get us closer to God. Only true repentance leads to faith in God.

The second part of the verse in Hebrews says that, after repentance, we must move on to *"faith toward God."* Placing our faith in God is another elementary, foundational principle of our Christian lives:

> *Therefore, leaving the discussion of the elementary principles of Christ, let us go on to perfection, not laying again the foundation of...faith toward God...* (Hebrews 6:1 NKJV).

What is faith? It is something that happens in the heart that produces a transformation in our lives. We cannot just make a profession of Christ in the realm of our minds. Faith toward God produces a change in our hearts. We are moved out of our sin and into His righteousness by our faith. The Bible literally defines *faith* in Hebrews 11:1:

Now faith is being sure of what we hope for and certain of what we do not see.

Faith involves believing first and then seeing. As Christians, we live and act as if we have already seen the Lord because we have confidence in God—we have placed our faith in Him. But of course, God is not visible to the naked eye. He is visible only to the eye of faith. We believe even though we do not "see" in the physical sense.

God called Abraham "a father of many nations" long before he had a son. The Bible says that Abraham *"in hope believed"* (Rom. 4:18) that this promise would come to pass. He did not wait until he saw the physical evidence before he believed by faith.

Faith is a *"gift of God"* (Eph. 2:8), and God uses His divine spoon to give you a *"measure of faith,"* according to Romans 12:3.

Therefore, the question is not, "How do I get faith?" but, "How do I exercise the faith that God has already given me?" All of us have faith in something. We may have faith in our ability to drive our car or faith that the ceiling in our home will not fall down. Some people have faith in their abilities, while others have faith in their philosophies. As Christians, our faith must be focused exclusively on the living God—in Jesus Christ.

WE RECEIVE JESUS BY FAITH ALONE

How do we receive Christ as Lord? By faith. How do we live out our Christian life each day? By faith. Hebrews 11:6 tells us,

And without faith it is impossible to please God, because anyone who comes to Him must believe that He exists and that He rewards those who earnestly seek Him.

Faith is our first response to God. We put our trust in Christ by faith and faith alone. We cannot depend on *our* abilities. We must depend on *His* abilities. If the world-renowned evangelist, Billy Graham, depended on his own works to be in right standing with God, he'd never make it, because God's standard is perfection. You see, even a great man of God like Billy Graham has not been perfect. No one is perfect except Jesus Christ. That's why we have to repent from trying to gain God's acceptance by our own morality or good works. Our efforts to "try harder" at being a better student, a better spouse, or a stronger Christian witness can never gain for us more acceptance from God. Placing our faith in God is the only way to please Him. We place our faith in the living God and serve Him for one reason, *because He is God.* He is worthy of our praise and our complete allegiance.

Since we have embraced Christ by faith, we must hold fast and not be sidetracked. When we receive Jesus as our Lord and put our faith in Him, we find that our lives are no longer filled solely with our own thoughts and desires, as our lives had been before we came to Christ. Things have changed! Christ is now actually living in us. Galatians 2:20 says,

> *Christ lives in me. The life I live in the body, I live by faith in the Son of God, who loved me and gave Himself for me.*

Why is this so important? Because when I realize that Christ lives in me, I begin to see life from a different perspective. I see it as it really is. Christ lives in me. And the same Holy Spirit who dwelt in Jesus Christ two thousand years ago, who gave Him the power to live a supernatural life, is also in me, enabling me to live a supernatural life. His power will lead me on.

PUT YOURSELF TO THE TEST

Remember, faith is not based on our outward appearance or on what we do; although true faith will result in changed behavior. We may be church members, give money in the offering every week, help other people, and even give our lives in service to others. But, as we learned earlier, these good works do not make a person a true Christian, although a Christian will certainly do such things. People who look like Christians on the outside, but have no real spiritual life on the inside, are disappointing counterfeits.

Sometimes counterfeit Christians and genuine Christians look so much alike on the outside that you can hardly tell the difference. God wants us to take stock of our own lives to be completely sure that we are genuine. The Scriptures tell us,

Examine yourselves to see whether you are in the faith; test yourselves. Do you not realize that Christ Jesus is in you— unless, of course, you fail the test (2 Corinthians 13:5).

We must look closely at ourselves and compare what we are to what the Scriptures say a Christian must be. Police officers who are trained to spot counterfeit money spend much time in training and studying the real thing. When we study the real thing, the Bible, and allow the Holy Spirit to teach us, we will know the difference between reality and the counterfeit. The Bible tells us that the Holy Spirit will guide us into all truth: *"But when He, the Spirit of truth, comes, He will guide you into all truth"* (John 16:13). The Holy Spirit convicts us in order to teach, correct, and guide us into truth.

One day a friend gave me a candy bar. Little did I know that he had eaten the real candy bar and carefully replaced it with a piece of wood. When I opened the wrapper, I discovered his clever trick!

Every Christian must examine himself to determine if his salvation is a present reality or if it is a counterfeit.

RIGHTEOUS THROUGH FAITH

How do we know that we are right with God and not a counterfeit Christian? Romans 3:22 says that we are righteous only through faith in Jesus Christ: "*This righteousness from God comes through faith in Jesus Christ to all who believe....*"

Righteousness is our right standing with God. A *righteousness consciousness* means *being constantly conscious, or thinking about, our right standing with God through faith in Jesus Christ.*

Romans 4:3 tells us clearly, "*Abraham believed God, and it was credited to him as righteousness.*" The word *accounted* literally means "credited."[1] The Lord credits our account with righteousness when we believe Him. Imagine someone depositing money in your account at the bank each week. You'd say, "I don't deserve this." But your bank account would continue to grow whether you deserved it or not! That is exactly what God does. The Bible says that if we believe God, like Abraham, the Lord puts *righteousness* into our account. So, being right with God does not depend on our performance; it depends on our faith in Jesus Christ—our trust in Him.

When we begin to confess the truth of our righteousness by faith, do you know what happens? The Lord provides for our needs! "*But seek first His kingdom and His righteousness, and all these things will be given to you as well*" (Matt. 6:33). But God provides for our needs because we are His children through faith in Jesus Christ. God makes us righteousness through faith in Jesus. God has accepted us. When we seek Him, He will provide for us.

I grew up on a family farm in Pennsylvania as an only son. Both my family and I expected that I would eventually take over the family farm, with the possibility of turning it into an even more profitable enterprise. A few years after I was married, I realized that the Lord was calling me to give up this opportunity so that I could serve as the pastor of a new church, without the promise of a great salary. As I have continued to seek first His Kingdom and His righteousness during the past 29 years, the Lord has provided for us again and again in amazing ways.

New Christians often make the mistake of relying too much on their feelings. One day they *feel* close to God, and the next day they don't *feel* Him. We cannot trust our feelings. We have to trust the truth of the Word of God. When we are tempted to be discouraged or depressed, we must make the decision, in Jesus' name, to replace those thoughts with the thoughts that God thinks about us. See yourself as God sees you. Look at others as God looks at them. Seek first His Kingdom and His righteousness, and the Lord will respond by adding all that you need.

BEWARE OF A SIN CONSCIOUSNESS

Some people have the opposite mentality of a *righteousness consciousness*; they have a *sin consciousness*. When people have a sin consciousness, they constantly are aware of, or thinking about, their tendency toward failure and sin. While it is true that, by ourselves, we cannot obey God, the Bible says that we can trust His competence (have faith in His strength to see us through):

Such confidence as this is ours through Christ before God. Not that we are competent in ourselves to claim anything for ourselves, but our competence comes from God. He has made us competent as ministers of a new covenant—not of the letter but of the Spirit; for the letter kills, but the Spirit gives life (2 Corinthians 3:4-6).

It is only by God's competence that we are able to do anything. We have absolutely no chance of obeying God with our own strength. We must have faith in God's strength. Every time we look to ourselves to try to "pull ourselves up by our own bootstraps," we begin to live with a sin consciousness. Sin consciousness turns our thoughts inward. We depend on our own abilities and become proud when we succeed, or we feel like a failure when we do not succeed. Instead, we must look to Jesus, who gives us strength and peace.

It's like this. If you're in the hospital and they take out your almost-ruptured appendix, what are you going to concentrate on? The pain? The stitches? Or are you going to say, "Praise God! The poison's being removed. I'm being healed in Jesus' name!" We choose to think of one or the other, the pain or the healing. If we keep our eyes on Jesus and on His righteousness, then God is free to allow the abundant life that He promised to permeate our lives.

I can promise you that, if you're a child of God, and if there is an area in your life where you are sinning, the Lord will tell you. He loves you that much. He will tell you through His Word, or He may bring people into your life to tell you. He will do whatever it takes to make sure that you know the truth. This way, you will look to Jesus and know that you are "righteous in Him." When we understand this principle and begin to live in the righteousness of God, we begin to live a life of victory. Whenever we look to ourselves instead of to Jesus for our righteousness, we begin to experience confusion and discouragement.

When I was a new believer in Christ, I went through a season where I had feelings of not being right with God. The more I tried to feel righteous, the worse I felt. Then one day I realized that there is nothing that I can do to make myself feel righteous. I was righteous because God said I was righteous in His Word. I began to speak every day to myself, "I am righteous through faith in Jesus Christ," and my feelings began to catch up with the truth that I was speaking. Feelings of confusion and discouragement were replaced with feelings of confidence in my right relationship with Christ.

PLANT YOUR RIGHTEOUSNESS SEEDS

Did you ever wake up on a holiday and find your alarm ringing in the morning at its normal time? You wake up and tell yourself that you have to go to work, then you realize, "This is a holiday. I can sleep in!" You awaken to the truth.

The Bible encourages us to *"awake to righteousness."* I can witness to others about Jesus. I can be a man or woman of God. I can go to work and enjoy it. I can love my parents. I can raise a family for the Lord, regardless of my present circumstances. I can take a step of faith. I can be victorious. I am righteous through faith in Jesus Christ. You awaken to the God-given truth that you can live righteously and victoriously by the grace of God.

Awake to righteousness, and do not sin, for some do not have the knowledge of God (1 Corinthians 15:34a NKJV).

I once heard the story of a rescue operation of two men in a boat that had capsized. A helicopter dropped a rope and the first man held onto the rope to be pulled up into the helicopter. But the second man cried out, "Oh, don't do that! It's extremely dangerous to hang onto a rope tied to the bottom of a helicopter." Both men had a choice. They could either hang onto the rope and be pulled to safety or lose their lives. Either we trust God and receive His righteousness by faith instead of trusting in dead works, or we die spiritually. That's how important this truth is. Righteousness through faith in Jesus is the only way out.

Again, I want to emphasize that righteousness through faith has nothing to do with the way we feel. It is based on the Word of God and His ability, not on us and our limited ability to "be good." Sometimes it takes time to see the results of living in righteousness by faith. It is like a certain kind of gigantic tropical species of bamboo plant. Initially, the new shoots grow slowly, but suddenly the growth rate increases rapidly and may reach nearly 60 cm (24 inches) per day!

So, do not give up. Plant your "righteousness consciousness seeds" and say, "I'm righteous by faith in Jesus." You may not feel any different initially, but you must keep saying it because you know it is true. *"Faith comes by hearing, and hearing by the Word of God"* (Rom. 10:17). One day the Word of God is going to bear fruit in your life, and it's going to grow and completely change your life.

Don't be afraid to talk to yourself to encourage yourself in your faith. I talk to myself all the time. The Bible says that David talked to himself; he *"encouraged himself in the Lord"* (1 Sam. 30:6 KJV). Another time, in Psalm 103:1, we see David talking to himself, *"Praise the Lord, O my soul; all my inmost being, praise His holy name."* We should be doing the same thing. I encourage you to get up in the morning and say, "I am righteous through faith in Jesus. I am a man or woman of God. I can do all things through Christ who strengthens me today" (see Phil. 4:13).

LOOK TO JESUS

Remember how satan deceived Adam and Eve in the Garden? He continues to deceive and blind the minds of people today. The devil hates to see people put their trust and faith in the Lord. He knows that, if he can get people to look at fear, poverty, disease, and their circumstances, they will become defeated and depressed. Some days I don't spend enough time with God, even though I know that the Lord has called me to seek His face, read His Word, and look to Him. It is often at these times that the devil comes to me to say, "It's all over because you failed. Now God can't use you."

Instead of listening to his lies, I immediately pray, "Lord, I believe what your Word says about me. I repent of 'missing the mark' today, and by your grace, Lord, I am going to be obedient to You."

There is a toy that you can find in some department stores. It's a big, tall toy on a heavy base. When you push it over, it always pops back up. That's the way God wants us to be as Christians. We need to say, "I will not listen to the lies of the devil. If I fall, I will get up in Jesus' name and move on with my God."

A man of God once said, "Look around and get distressed. Look within and get depressed. Look to Jesus and be at rest." We must trust God in faith to truly please Him. The Lord has great plans for our lives according to Jeremiah 29:11:

"For I know the plans I have for you," declares the Lord, "plans to prosper you and not to harm you, plans to give you hope and a future."

Yes, He is talking about you and me. Our God is thinking of us and cares about our futures.

ENDNOTES

1. W. E. Vine, *Vine's Expository Dictionary* (Old Tappan, NJ: Fleming H. Revell Company, 1981), s.v. "Accounted."

2. "Bamboo," *Microsoft Encarta Online Encyclopedia*, 2001, http://encarta.msn.com.

FAITH IN GOD
REFLECTION QUESTIONS

1. What helps you to recognize the difference between the real and the counterfeit Christian?

2. What is a "sin consciousness"? Why is having a negative attitude a sign of weak faith?

3. What are some ways that the devil lies to you?

4. What are some ways that you can "awake to righteousness"?

Chapter 7

THE POTENT MIXTURE: FAITH AND THE WORD

IS THE BIBLE THE TRUE WORD OF GOD?

In this chapter, we will discover how faith and God's Word, the Bible, are a powerful mix to help us live the abundant life that Christ wants to give us. But first, let's briefly look at why we believe the Bible is the true Word of God. Some of the many books today that claim to be the Word of God are the Qur'an, *The Book of Mormon, The Bhagavad Gita,* and the Bible. Christians believe that the Bible is the Word of God and the source of truth to live by. What is the evidence proving the authority and divine origin of the Bible?

The Bible proclaims to be the Word of God: "*All Scripture is inspired by God*" (2 Tim. 3:16 NASB). Another version translates *theopnuestos* (inspired) as "God-breathed" (NIV). The writers of Scripture were supernaturally guided to write what God wanted written.

Holy men of God spoke as they were moved by the Holy Spirit (2 Peter 1:20-21 NKJV).

Jesus taught that the Scripture is God's inspired Word, even to the smallest detail:

I tell you the truth, until heaven and earth disappear, not the smallest letter, not the least stroke of a pen, will by any means disappear from the Law until everything is accomplished (Matthew 5:18).

Although skeptics have tried to destroy the authority of the Bible, it has remained the most well-known book in the history of the world and has proven itself true again and again. The Bible was written over a period of 1500 years by over 40 different authors from all walks of life, in many different countries, addressing hundreds of issues, and yet it remains unified in its message from God. The unity alone is an amazing proof of the divine inspiration and authority of the Bible.

MIXING FAITH AND THE WORD

We need to take God's Word and mix it with faith. Hearing God's Word alone will not change us, but (by faith) acting on it will. The book of Hebrews tells us that *"the message they* [the Israelites in the wilderness] *heard was of no value to them, because those who heard did not combine it with faith"* (Heb. 4:2).

Combining God's Word with faith is a supernatural mix that causes something powerful to happen. It reminds me of epoxy glue. When the two ingredients of epoxy glue are mixed together, something powerful happens, and you can bond together all kinds of materials with it.

When I was a young boy, I really wanted a chemistry set. My parents never got me one. I think they were afraid that I would blow the roof off the house! However, I improvised by making my own experiments. One day I mixed baking soda and vinegar and discovered that they make a great explosion. Baking soda and vinegar by themselves are not explosive, but when you mix them, an explosive chemical reaction occurs.

In the same way, you can trigger a spiritual explosion in your life when you mix the Word of God with your faith and say, "I'm going to believe God's Word and act on it." True faith rises up in your heart, and you experience the abundant life that Jesus promised. You are not basing your life on your own righteousness, but instead, on the righteousness that comes by faith in Jesus Christ and His Word.

One day an emotionally depressed woman came to a wise believer for advice. She explained that her daughter was involved in immorality. He gave her simple advice, "You need to start seeing yourself and your daughter as God sees you. Rather than being despondent about her situation, see her at the cross of Jesus. Confess the truth of God's Word for her life."

A few months later, the woman and her daughter came back, beaming from ear to ear. The woman explained: "I prayed and began to see my daughter from God's perspective. She had been living with a man who was not her husband, and one day she woke up so depressed that she decided to take her own life. But, first, she came home to see me. My family and I received her with joy. She received so much love from our family that she made a decision to give her life to Jesus. Why? Because we saw her at the cross through Jesus' eyes of love." This family placed their faith in the Word of God instead of their feelings or circumstances. The Lord wants you and me to do the same.

JESUS AND HIS WORD ARE ONE

The best way to serve Jesus Christ and know His will for our lives is simply to live in obedience to His Word—the Scriptures. You see, Jesus and His Word are one. Revelation 19:13 says, "...*His name is the Word of God.*"

When I travel, my wife often leaves me notes in my luggage. I love to read her notes because it's the same as if she were talking to me. When God's Word tells me that He loves me or commands me to do something, it is the same as if Jesus were speaking to me audibly in His own words. We can constantly live under the Lordship of Jesus by listening to what He says—as expressed in His Word. Jesus tells us,

The words I have spoken to you are spirit and they are life (John 6:63b).

True Christians have chosen to live their lives in complete obedience to the Word of God. His words are spirit and life to us. The Bible leads us directly into God's will, and it keeps us from living according to our own desires instead of His desires. You need to read God's Word every day and confess Jesus Christ as your Lord so that you can live in victory. God's Word renews your mind.

Do not conform any longer to the pattern of this world, but be transformed by the renewing of your mind. Then you will be able to test and approve what God's will is—His good, pleasing and perfect will (Romans 12:2).

When we renew our minds daily with the Word of God and obey the truth found there, it not only helps us to know Jesus better, it also sets us free. When we obey the words that He has spoken to us in the Scriptures and the words that He speaks to us by His Holy Spirit, we are obeying God. That is why the Scriptures are so important.

If I feel like holding a grudge against someone and yet see in the Scriptures that, if I do not forgive others, God will not forgive me (see Matt. 6:14-15), I come to a crossroads in my life. Either I choose my way or God's way. We must trust and obey God's Word to renew our minds and change us.

RELEASE FAITH, CONFESS THE WORD

You can release your faith by confessing God's Word with your mouth, according to Romans 10:9-10:

That if you confess with your mouth, "Jesus is Lord," and believe in your heart that God raised Him from the dead, you will be saved. For it is with your heart that you believe and are justified, and it is with your mouth that you confess and are saved.

We are saved when we believe the truth from the Word of God in our hearts and confess it with our mouths. When we receive Jesus, we receive the Gospel or *good news*. God's Word, the Bible, is filled with God's good news.

Being saved does not only mean that we go to Heaven, as wonderful as that is. It also means that we are being healed and set free inside. It means that we can be set free emotionally, financially, mentally, and in every other area of our lives. The key is to believe the Word and confess it so that faith can mix with God's Word and release mighty miracles in our lives.

I thank God every day that I'm righteous through faith in Jesus Christ. I'm thankful for His Word, and I'm thankful for what He's done in my life. I know that I am right with God, not because of the good works that I do, but because of faith in Jesus Christ.

When I became a new Christian, I began to read the Word of God day by day. I started to think and act differently because my mind was being renewed by the Word of God. Faith rose up in me

91

as a result of God's Word, just like the Scriptures promise in Romans 10:17:

> *Consequently, faith comes from hearing the message, and the message is heard through the word of Christ.*

SEE FAITH COMING

I have a friend who served as a pastor in India for many years. He said, "In Eastern cultures, we see the Bible differently than you do. We see in pictures. We read in the Scriptures that faith comes by hearing and hearing by the Word of God, and we really see faith coming! We confess it because God says it is so, and we see it coming with our spiritual eyes."

I believe the Lord wants us to see what happens when we take the Bible seriously and speak the truth to ourselves. We will "see faith coming." Most of the time, people wait to feel their faith with their emotions, but this is going about it backwards.

I grew up with a lot of insecurities. In fact, I was even afraid to make eye contact with people. But after I received Jesus as the Lord of my life, I realized that the Christ who lives inside me is not insecure! I began to talk to myself each day, telling myself that Christ lived inside of me. And the feelings of insecurity began to vanish because faith came when I spoke the truth to myself.

Imagine a train running down a track. Let's compare the engine that pulls the train to the *Word of God*. The next car is *our faith*. And the last car, the caboose, is our *feelings* or *our emotions*.

When we place our faith in the Word of God, our feelings or emotions will always follow like a caboose. However, if we place our faith in our feelings first, we will be frustrated, and the enemy will begin to discourage us. We must place our faith in the Word of God first. Then the "feelings of faith" will follow. Faith is not a feeling. It is a mighty, living force released in our lives when we choose to hear and confess God's Word daily.

> *For the word of God is living and active. Sharper than any double-edged sword, it penetrates even to dividing soul and spirit, joints and marrow; it judges the thoughts and attitudes of the heart* (Hebrews 4:12).

The Word of God causes us to begin to think like Jesus thinks; it releases the Lord's power so that we can know the difference between our own thoughts (in the soul) and the thoughts that the Lord has placed in our spirits.

MEDITATE ON GOD'S WORD

To grow spiritually, we must read and meditate on the Word of God each day. In this way, our minds become renewed. We must fill our minds with the truth of the Word of God, or we will be side-tracked by the philosophies of the world system around us that are completely against the truth of Jesus Christ. Exercising faith in God involves reading God's Word and obeying it.

How do we meditate on the Word of God? To meditate simply means to roll something around over and over again in our minds. Joshua 1:8 tells us,

> *Do not let this Book of the Law depart from your mouth; meditate on it day and night, so that you may be careful to do everything written in it. Then you will be prosperous and successful.*

Cows have multiple stomachs. They will fill their stomachs with grass, and then spend the rest of the day lying under a shade tree "chewing their cud." Food is passed from one stomach to the other in stages as they intermittently regurgitate it and then chew it again. We could liken this process to meditating on the Word of God. We need to read the Word and then write portions of it down and bring it back various times throughout the day to memorize it and meditate on it (chew on it!).

When I gave my life to Christ, I regularly wrote down a verse of Scripture that had special significance to me on an index card. Throughout the day, I pulled out the card to memorize it and meditate on its meaning. I literally "rolled around" God's Word in my mind until it became a part of me. During the first few years as a new Christian, I memorized hundreds of verses of Scripture this way.

There is a big difference between meditation on God's Word and the meditation practiced with some yoga techniques or by Hindu gurus and Buddhist monks. These religious leaders and various modern-day new age cults instruct their followers to meditate with one primary goal: *to empty their minds.* In this disconnection between the body and spirit, or altered state of consciousness, a doorway to the demonic could be opened to the human soul. In sharp contrast, God's Word encourages us to *fill our minds* with (meditate on) the Word of God. As we do so, the Holy Spirit illuminates the Word of God to our minds, and we are changed.

SPIRITUAL SOWING AND REAPING

God has called you and me to sow His Word by praying in alignment with its truth and by speaking it to others. Jesus talked about sowers of God's Word in the Gospel of Mark:

The farmer I talked about is anyone who brings God's message to others...the good soil represents the hearts of those who truly accept God's message and produce a plentiful harvest for God—thirty, sixty, or even a hundred times as much as was planted...(Mark 4:14,20 TLB).

When we sow the seed of the Word of God, God works through it to produce a supernatural spiritual crop. It may not happen the first day, or the first week, but it will happen.

As a young boy, I remember throwing a few watermelon seeds into our garden. Months later we had watermelons everywhere! When we sow the Word of God through prayer and through confessing the truth, we will see a mighty crop, a bountiful harvest come forth for God.

You sow dynamic spiritual seeds into lives through prayer and encouragement every time you pray for loved ones or for yourself. Remember that God has promised that He will produce a crop through the seeds that we sow.

While traveling with a young man who was not yet a Christian, I began to sow spiritual seeds into his life. I simply told him, "God has a call on your life, and I believe you are going to be a man of God. God is going to use you." Months later, he told me that he received Christ into his life and reminded me of the "seeds of truth" that I sowed into his life months before.

The whole world is God's spiritual garden, and He wants us to sow seeds of life everywhere we go. Let's plant spiritual seeds by faith into people's lives. Then we can do what farmers do every year—pray and expect the seeds to grow.

THE POTENT MIXTURE: FAITH AND THE WORD
REFLECTION QUESTIONS

1. Give an example of a time when you not only heard God's Word but also acted on it in faith.

2. How is God's Word renewing your mind today?

3. Describe a time in your life when you "saw faith coming."

4. What are some ways that you meditate on God's Word?

Chapter 8

WE CAN LIVE VICTORIOUSLY

A BATTLE TO BE FOUGHT

Why do so many people seem to be uninterested in the things of God? Many do not believe in Jesus because they are spiritually blinded by the enemy:

And even if our gospel is veiled, it is veiled to those who are perishing. The god of this age has blinded the minds of unbelievers, so that they cannot see the light of the gospel of the glory of Christ, who is the image of God (2 Corinthians 4:3-4).

Satan not only tries to hide the truth of the Gospel from us, he is ready to do battle with us once we become Christians. The walk of the Christian is described as spiritual warfare, and we must be equipped to fight. According to Ephesians 6:12, there is a battle being waged for our souls. This battle is not with people, but with the demons of hell:

For our struggle is not against flesh and blood, but against the rulers, against the authorities, against the powers of this dark world and against the spiritual forces of evil in the heavenly realms (Ephesians 6:12).

Prayer and the declaration of the Word of God break down these demonic hindrances so that we can receive the Word of God and the life-giving conviction of the Holy Spirit. A friend and I went to pray for a man who had cancer. My friend, along with the man's wife and daughter-in-law, had been praying for his salvation for many years, but he was unwilling to receive Christ. After entering his home, I felt impressed to share my testimony with him. About 30 minutes later, he was ready to receive Jesus Christ as the Lord of his life. We rejoiced, knowing that the true battle was won in prayer prior to that day by those who loved him. In prayer, his friend, wife, and daughter-in-law had battled the evil forces that had spiritually blinded their loved one, allowing the light of the Gospel to penetrate.

Unbelief comes from the devil and from all of his hordes of demonic angels. We live in a spiritual world and must fight spiritual battles: "*Therefore put on the full armor of God, so that when the day of evil comes, you may be able to stand your ground....take...the sword of the Spirit, which is the word of God*" (Eph. 6:13a,17b). The sword of the Spirit that we use to conquer the devil is the Word of God. As we learned earlier, we mix the Word of God with faith and sow the seeds. God promises that we will get a good crop and be victorious in our battles.

COMPLETE IN SPIRIT, SOUL, AND BODY

There is another battlefield: it is in our minds. My mind is bombarded with many thoughts every day, some not from God. It is important to understand that temptation is not sin because *every Christian is tempted* (see 1 Cor. 10:13; Heb. 4:15). Temptation becomes sin when we think about it and allow it to gain control of our thoughts and actions. How do we handle the wrong thoughts that come to our minds? We speak the Word of God and rebuke the devil in the name of Jesus. Then we go on, knowing that we are righteous by faith in Jesus Christ.

As Christians, we need to daily purify ourselves from every sin that threatens to contaminate us. The Bible teaches us that we are made up of body, soul, and spirit (see 1 Thess. 5:23). Before you were a Christian, your body, soul, and spirit were polluted by sin. But as a believer, you are made holy:

May God Himself, the God of peace, sanctify you through and through. May your whole spirit, soul and body be kept blameless at the coming of our Lord Jesus Christ (1 Thessalonians 5:23).

If you and I sat down and talked face to face, you would not see all of me. What you would see is my body. My spirit is the part of me that communicates with God. My soul is a composite of my mind, my will, and my emotions.

Like me, you have the three aspects of spirit, soul, and body. When we are born again by the Spirit of God, we receive Jesus as Lord, and our spirits are instantly born again (see John 3:3-8). We are brand-new inside. Do our bodies change? Absolutely. Look closely at people who are filled with Jesus; they have a sense of the Lord's peace on their countenances. They "glow" because of the Lord's presence, and their faces shine with the glory of God.

What happens to the soul? The soul doesn't change instantaneously. It begins to be renewed as we read, hear, and meditate on the Word of God. The Bible tells us to

...be transformed by the renewing of your mind. Then you will be able to test and approve what God's will is—His good, pleasing and perfect will (Romans 12:2).

To a certain degree, we are all products of our past. We learned to think a certain way (man's way) about the main issues of life. The Word of God renews our minds to see life from *God's perspective* and to reap the benefits that come with divine wisdom (see Josh. 1:8).

By meditating on the Word of God, we begin to see ourselves from the Lord's perspective instead of from our own. A new Christian will find that his soul (mind, will, and emotions) begins to catch up with what happened in his spirit when he received Jesus as his Lord. Gradually, he starts to "think like God" (he thinks according to the guidelines revealed in God's Word), instead of according to his past way of thinking.

When we lay our past (and present) before the Lord, His peace will stand guard at the door of our hearts and minds and change us:

And the peace of God, which transcends all understanding, will guard your hearts and your minds in Christ Jesus. Finally, brothers, whatever is true, whatever is noble, whatever is right, whatever is pure, whatever is lovely, whatever is admirable—if anything is excellent or praiseworthy—think about such things (Philippians 4:7-8).

If we fix our minds on the holy things in life, God's peace will prevent the heartaches of this world from wrecking our lives. The Lord knows that we are a work in progress, and He will change us daily—body, soul, and spirit.

YOU ARE A NEW CREATION

As soon as you were born again—you received Jesus as Lord—a miracle happened inside of you. You became a brand-new person.

You are a new creation in Jesus Christ. The Bible says in Second Corinthians 5:17,

> *Therefore, if anyone is in Christ, he is a new creation; the old has gone, the new has come!*

An elephant becoming a butterfly would be no greater miracle! Yes, there is an indescribable miracle that happens inside of us as we live by faith in Jesus. Remember, putting our faith in Jesus means that we cannot trust ourselves or our good works. In Second Corinthians 1:9-10, Paul was imprisoned and in very dire circumstances. Still, he urged the Corinthian church not to trust in themselves but to trust in God who alone has the power to deliver:

> *...that we might not rely on ourselves but on God, who raises the dead. He has delivered us from such a deadly peril, and He will deliver us. On Him we have set our hope that He will continue to deliver us.*

Faith is believing and trusting in God and God alone. It's not a matter of "turning over a new leaf" or just changing some of our old ways of doing things. No, a miracle has happened inside. We know that it has happened because God's Word says that it has. We know by faith in the Word of God that we are new creations in Jesus Christ. Christianity is walking by faith, not by sight! We are righteous only by faith in Jesus Christ, and He makes us new day by day.

SET FREE

When we join God's family, we are set free from the power of sin over our lives; we are set free from its guilt. Jesus tells us in John 8:31-32,

...if you hold to My teaching, you are really My disciples. Then you will know the truth, and the truth will set you free.

The first part of that verse says that we must continue in God's Word—love it, keep it, and walk in it—and as a result, we shall know the truth and experience freedom. No one is truly free until the power of sin has been rendered inoperative as we consider ourselves dead to sin and alive to God (see Rom. 6:11). The Bible tells us that we are adopted into God's family:

For you did not receive a spirit that makes you a slave again to fear, but you received the Spirit of sonship. And by Him we cry, "Abba, Father" (Romans 8:15).

Every person living in sin is subject to fear because he is guilty. His conscience will trouble him. But a Christian does not have this fear because he has been adopted as a child into God's family (see John 1:12; Eph. 1:5; Gal. 4:5).

False guilt is something that feels like guilt, but it is really just shame. It is the leftover negative feelings from our sinful past. False guilt causes us to hang on to our feelings of being dirty and sinful, even after we have confessed our sins and God has forgiven us. Before I received Jesus as my Lord, I experienced genuine guilt over my sins. Yet even after I received the Lord, the guilt continued, although I was totally forgiven from God's perspective. Then I read First John 1:9:

If we confess our sins, He is faithful and just and will forgive us our sins and purify us from all unrighteousness.

From that moment on, I stopped living by past experiences, feelings, and fears. I started living by the Word of God, and the guilt left. I knew that I was forgiven because the Bible told me so! I remembered that God had *"removed my sins as far as the east is from the west"* (Ps. 103:12). I was safe from all condemnation for my sins. It was as if they had not been committed at all. That is how freely God forgives when we place our trust in Him.

THE DEVIL CONDEMNS; GOD CONVICTS

The devil will tell us that it is a long way back to God when we sin. He will try to make us believe that God will never use us again. But we now know better. If we sin, we must repent (we stop it, and we change our direction). The Lord forgives us, and we start with a new, clean slate.

Sometimes restitution has to follow repentance. This is putting things right with people we have wronged. If someone repents from shoplifting, he needs to pay it back. Although he is forgiven the moment that he confesses his sin, he needs to take a step of obedience and restore what was stolen. When Zacchaeus repented for running a crooked tax collection agency, he told the Lord that he would restore four times what he stole (see Luke 19:8-9).

Some time after I received Jesus Christ as my Lord, I was convicted by the Holy Spirit when I remembered that I had deceived a classmate in high school. Another friend and I were gambling with him and had "rigged it" so that he always lost. I wrote to the classmate, explained what had happened, and asked him for forgiveness, returning the money that I had taken from him with interest. A few weeks later, I received a return letter saying that he forgave me and thanking me for writing. I did not restore what I had taken so that I could be forgiven; I restored it because I *was* forgiven.

The devil condemns us, but God convicts us of our sin. What is the difference between the two? Condemnation brings doubt, fear, unbelief, and hopelessness. Satan condemns us to bring us down and

103

destroy our faith. God convicts us to restore us to righteousness and faith. He always corrects us to build us up, and His conviction always brings hope and a way of escape:

> *No temptation has seized you except what is common to man. And God is faithful; He will not let you be tempted beyond what you can bear. But when you are tempted, He will also provide a way out so that you can stand up under it* (1 Corinthians 10:13).

Don't accept condemnation from satan or from other people.

> *Therefore, there is now no condemnation for those who are in Christ Jesus, because through Christ Jesus the law of the Spirit of life set me free from the law of sin and death* (Romans 8:1-2).

Jesus Christ has made you free! You are free from the law of sin and death. He has made you righteous by faith in Him.

YOU CAN HAVE A FULL LIFE

Christ wants to give us a full, abundant life, and He tells us so when He says,

> *...I have come that they might have life, and that they may have it more abundantly* (John 10:10 NKJV).

The term *abundant life* is translated from the Greek word *zoe* which means "the very nature of God and source of life."[1] The abundant life, then, is life filled with the very nature of God inside of us. This life is abundant in quantity and quality—overflowing life. That is the kind of life that God has prepared for us as His children.

Christ lives in us to help us live victoriously and fully: "*Christ lives in me. The life I live in the body, I live by faith in the Son of God, who loved me and gave Himself for me*" (Gal. 2:20b). I keenly remember when this truth was made real to me while working on the family farm. I was herding livestock and frustrated by my lack of ability to accomplish the task. Then I prayed for God's wisdom rather than trusting in my own strength. As I confessed the truth of "Christ living in me," I was energized to complete my job! I received a clear realization that the Lord lived in me and that He wanted me to depend on His strength and His alone.

Do you want to know what the Lord's will is for your life? Of course you do! Trust completely that Jesus is in control of your life and wants to give you the strength that you need to persevere. Begin to renew your mind daily with the Word of God, and you will discover the Lord's plans for your life. If our minds are like a painter's canvas, God's Word is the paint. God, the Holy Spirit, is like a paintbrush who wants to paint a clear picture concerning His will for our lives, but we need to have enough paint available for Him to draw us a clear picture.

Briefly, here are a few things to do to grow spiritually. We should worship God on a daily basis (see John 4:23-24). We need to pray to Him and read the Bible. It is also important to worship with other Christians on a regular basis (see Heb. 10:24-25). We need to find a local church and develop relationships with the people there. In addition, we should share the Gospel with others who need to hear (see Matt. 28:19-20). When we do these things, we can expect our lifestyle to change. We will begin to experience the abundant life that Jesus came to give us.

YOU ARE ACCEPTED

Ephesians 1:6 tells us that we are *"accepted in the Beloved"* (God's family). When we are born again, we actually become a part of God's family. The Creator of the universe wants you and me to be in His family! First John 3:1 says,

> *How great is the love the Father has lavished on us, that we should be called children of God!*

Think of it. You really are a child of the living God when you receive Jesus Christ by faith. You are righteous. No matter what you have done today or yesterday, you are right with God as soon as you believe that God's Word is true and say, "Lord, I know I'm righteous only because of my faith that You've given me—faith in Jesus Christ. Thank You, God, that I am righteous not by my works but by faith in Jesus Christ today."

We all have a need to be accepted. I have felt misunderstood, left out, and rejected many times in my life. In my first year at school, I was one of those kids who was usually the last one picked to play baseball with my schoolmates. It really hurt.

How about you? Can you remember times in your life when you felt all alone? Here is the good news. We are not alone! We can be secure in the fact that God loves us. When I realized that Jesus Christ accepted me just the way I was, a new security came into my life. And now, I can accept others because I know that God has accepted me.

God has good plans for your life today. He wants you to reign in life through Jesus Christ because

> *...those who receive God's abundant provision of grace and of the gift of righteousness reign in life through the one man, Jesus Christ* (Romans 5:17b).

Do not allow the enemy to get your focus off of Jesus and His righteousness. Refuse to be controlled by your feelings or circumstances. Rise up in faith and begin to reign in life through Jesus Christ and His righteousness. I have some good news for you: you don't have to wait. You can start today!

ENDNOTE

1. *The New Testament Greek Lexicon*, s.v. "Zoe," www.studylight. org/lex/grk/view.cgi?number=2222 (accessed 24 Sept 2008).

WE CAN LIVE VICTORIOUSLY
REFLECTION QUESTIONS

1. Describe a spiritual battle that you fought and won recently. How did God's Word aid you?

2. Explain in your own words what it means to be "in Christ." What is the evidence of being a new creation?

3. Think about a time that you have felt condemned rather than convicted of a sin. Explain the difference.

4. Name some of the things that you do that help you to experience an abundant life in Christ.

PART III

New Testament Baptisms

Chapter 9

BAPTISM
IN WATER

DOCTRINE OF BAPTISMS

Being baptized is one of the first steps that a new Christian should make. Baptism is an essential part of the spiritual foundation of a new Christian's life. When we think of baptism, we normally think of water baptism and its various modes—sprinkling, pouring, and immersion. But there really are more kinds of baptisms mentioned in God's Word than just water baptism. Let's look at Hebrews 6.

In addition to the foundational principles that we learned previously (*repentance from dead works* and *faith toward God*), Hebrews 6 lists yet another elementary principle—the doctrine of baptisms:

Therefore, leaving the discussion of the elementary principles of Christ, let us go on to perfection, not laying again the foundation of...the doctrine of baptisms...(Hebrews 6:1-2 NKJV).

Since this spiritual foundation is listed as plural—baptisms—it indicates that the Christian faith includes more than one kind of baptism. As we read through the New Testament, we discover that there are four distinct types of baptisms: baptism in water, baptism into the Body of Christ, baptism of fire, and baptism in the Holy

Spirit. Let's take a look at all four, starting with the Christian baptism in water.

A DEMONSTRATION OF OBEDIENCE

Water baptism, sometimes called *believer's baptism*, is for the purpose of identifying with Jesus. In the New Testament, once a person believed in Jesus for salvation, he or she was then baptized in water (see Mark 16:16; Acts 2:38; 8:12,36). Baptism is a sign of cleansing and forgiveness of sin—an act of faith and obedience. Jesus Himself introduced us to water baptism when He was baptized by John the Baptist.

John had been preaching a baptism of repentance for the forgiveness of sins (see Mark 1:4). When people repented of their sins, they were water baptized as the outward evidence that they had repented. Since it was an outward sign, it did not magically save them. The power in baptism was in the power of God, not in the water or the act itself.

"Then why," you may ask, "was Jesus baptized"? Jesus was without sin (see 1 Pet. 2:21-22); He did not need to show evidence of confessing and repenting of sin. John pondered the same question when Jesus came to him to be baptized. Jesus gave John the answer to his question when he said, *"Let it be so now; it is proper for us to do this to fulfill all righteousness"* (Matt. 3:15).

Jesus was setting an example for Christian believers to follow—not simply as evidence that they had confessed and repented of their sins, but *"to fulfill [complete] all righteousness."* Christian baptism is an outward act of obedience by which the believer fulfills the inward righteousness that he or she already has through faith in Christ's death and resurrection.

Jesus said that everywhere that the Gospel is preached, individuals will be saved when they believe. Baptism naturally followed: *"Whoever believes and is baptized will be saved..."* (Mark 16:16).

The natural succession and pattern of believing first and then being baptized is followed throughout the New Testament. Sometimes people ask, "I was baptized as an infant. Is infant baptism in the Bible?" Infant baptism is not mentioned in the Bible. The record of baptisms in the New Testament are of adults who were previously unbelievers. These believers were baptized after their belief and faith in Jesus. Since infants are incapable of exercising faith, and baptism is the outward sign of faith, it stands to reason that an infant is not eligible for baptism. Although there is not necessarily anything wrong with baptizing babies as a form of dedication to the Lord, according to Scripture, they should also be baptized after they believe as an outward sign of faith.

The key question to ask is this: have you been baptized since you've believed? The Bible teaches us to be baptized in water after we believe in Jesus. It is a sign of our faith.

A PUBLIC ANNOUNCEMENT

As a sign of our faith in Jesus, water baptism makes several bold statements. Let's look at these statements in the next four sections. First of all, the Bible tells us that water baptism is a public announcement of our decision to turn our backs on sin and live for Jesus Christ: *"...all should be baptized as a public announcement of their decision to turn their backs on sin"* (Mark 1:4 TLB).

Baptism is a public announcement that we have taken a clear stand for Jesus Christ. In the early Church, it was taken for granted that when someone turned his life over to Jesus Christ, his first step of obedience was water baptism:

> *Repent and be baptized, every one of you, in the name of Jesus Christ for the forgiveness of your sins...* (Acts 2:38).

When I was a youth worker, there were times when dozens of young people gave their lives to Jesus during a given week. We often baptized them the same day that they were born again. Some were baptized in swimming pools, others in rivers and ponds, and still others in bathtubs. These water baptisms were very meaningful, spiritual times. Baptisms can take place in varied settings, large or small. Some baptisms can be planned ahead and attended by friends and family, so that they can be a part of the celebration.

No matter what method or in what setting, new Christians are making a public statement by participating in the physical, outward sign of their salvation by being baptized. This act of faith is a decision that empowers Christians to fulfill the Great Commission to wholeheartedly make and baptize disciples.

> *Therefore go and make disciples of all nations, baptizing them in the name of the Father and of the Son and of the Holy Spirit, and teaching them to obey everything I have commanded you. And surely I am with you always, to the very end of the age* (Matthew 28:19-20).

SHOWS DEATH TO SIN, LIFE IN CHRIST

A second reason why water baptism is so important is that it shows that we are dead to sin and alive to Christ, according to Romans 6:4:

We were therefore buried with Him through baptism into death in order that, just as Christ was raised from the dead through the glory of the Father, we too may live a new life.

Water baptism is a sign of being buried to sin and resurrected to new life. Jesus was buried and resurrected two thousand years ago. We are buried with Him by baptism in a spiritual sense. We must be dead to ourselves before we can have new life. When we come to the cross, we die to our old way of living so that we can have the new resurrected life that God has promised.

When you go to a funeral and see a dead man, you know that he cannot respond to anything. He cannot be hurt physically or emotionally. He cannot feel pain. He is dead! When we are buried in Christ, our old nature no longer can do its own thing; it is dead. So then, spiritually speaking, our old life is dead.

Here's an example: Joe was a former gangster with the Mafia who gave his life to Jesus. His life was permanently changed. A few weeks after he gave his life to the Lord, one of his Mafia brothers called him on the phone and said, "Hey, is Joe there?"

Joe answered, "No, Joe died," and hung up the phone. The truth is, Joe *had* died. He was a brand-new Joe and was living a brand-new life. The old Joe was dead, a new Joe had come, and Jesus Christ now lived in him. Water baptism is a sign that we have died to self and, with the power of God's glory, now walk in a new life.

Sometimes people ask, "How should a person be baptized?" The Greek word for *baptize* is *baptizo*, which means "to immerse."[1] We encourage people to be immersed in the water. Going into the watery grave of baptism is symbolic of dying to self, of being buried and then resurrected as we come up out of the water.

You have been crucified with Christ. Your old "man" (evil nature) is dead. Through water baptism, you become dead to sin and alive to Christ.

ILLUSTRATES NEW TESTAMENT CIRCUMCISION

This brings us to a third statement that water baptism makes. Water baptism is a type of New Testament circumcision. In the Old Testament circumcision, when an infant boy was 8 days old, his foreskin was cut away as a sign of God's covenant to His people. It was a sign of faith, just as it is in the New Testament. Colossians 2:11-12 says that submitting to the watery grave of baptism, just like circumcision, shows that our old sin nature has been cut away, supernaturally:

> *In Him you were also circumcised, in the putting off of the sinful nature, not with a circumcision done by the hands of men but with the circumcision done by Christ, having been buried with Him in baptism and raised with Him through your faith in the power of God, who raised Him from the dead.*

The power of the sin nature that is inside of you and me—that old nature that says, "I want to do what I want to do"—is symbolically cut away when we're baptized in water. It's a New Testament circumcision.

Sometimes the devil comes and tries to tell us that we are still under bondage to the old habits of the past—lying, criticism, lust, hatred, anger, or whatever. That's like a former landlord coming to us and demanding that we pay rent for a house that we no longer live in. We can tell the devil, "You don't own me anymore. Go talk to my new landlord. His name is Jesus!"

When we are baptized in water, we are making a statement that the bondage of the past is broken. It's a supernatural work of God. Moses and the children of Israel were in bondage to the Egyptians, but when they came through the Red Sea, God's people were baptized and set free after coming through the water:

For I do not want you to be ignorant of the fact, brothers, that our forefathers were all under the cloud and that they all passed through the sea. They were all baptized into Moses in the cloud and in the sea (1 Corinthians 10:1-2).

Having trusted God, by faith in Jesus, for freedom from the bondage of our past, we are then baptized. We don't always feel that we are freed from bondage. That's why it's important that we know it by faith. We live by the truth of His Word, not by our emotions. I remember flying into my hometown of Lancaster, Pennsylvania, one time and feeling sure that we were going the wrong way. But we came into the right airport. The pilots were flying by the navigation equipment—and it was right. We should live our lives, not by every whim of our emotions, but according to God's navigation instrument, the Bible, which gives us the will of God.

Romans 6:14 says, "*For sin shall not be your master....*" Instead of seeing this Scripture as a law, see it as a promise. God says that sin shall not have power over me because I am buried with Him in baptism. The old me is dead. I am a brand-new person!

Our old, evil nature is rendered inoperative, and through water baptism, we experience New Testament circumcision. Romans 6:6 states,

For we know that our old self was crucified with Him so that the body of sin might be done away with, that we should no longer be slaves to sin.

The old has been cut away! We are living a new life with Jesus Christ inside of us.

SHOWS OBEDIENCE TO GOD

A fourth statement water baptism makes is that it shows we are obeying God. The Word of God instructs us to be baptized in water. We are exhorted to *"believe and be baptized"* (Mark 16:16). Water baptism symbolizes a spiritual cleansing, according to First Peter 3:21:

And this water symbolizes baptism that now saves you also— not the removal of dirt from the body but the pledge of a good conscience toward God. It saves you by the resurrection of Jesus Christ.

It is the cleansing of the heart, not the outward ceremony, that saves. Washing with water does little more than remove dirt. But being baptized shows that we are living with a clear conscience. We have an unwavering confidence in Jesus Christ. We are obeying the Lord in all that He has asked us to do, and it brings a tremendous freedom into our lives.

Sometimes people ask, "What about a deathbed conversion? If someone gives his heart to Jesus, dies two minutes later, and there is no time to baptize him, where does he spend eternity?" Remember, baptism does not save us. The blood of Jesus Christ saves us. Baptism is simply an act of obedience. After his profession of faith, the thief on the cross could not be water baptized, but Jesus said that He would see him in paradise (see Luke 23:40-43).

Nevertheless, according to the examples given in the Scriptures, and if we have the opportunity, we should be baptized as soon after conversion as possible. When Paul was in jail, the Philippian jailer gave his heart to Jesus. The jailer's whole household was baptized that night with water (see Acts 16:33). While Philip was walking down a road one day, he met an Ethiopian official sitting in his chariot and reading the Scriptures. Philip explained the good news about Jesus to him, and he was baptized as soon as they found some water (see Acts 8:38). Crispus and his household, and many other Corinthians, believed and were baptized immediately (see Acts 18:8).

Every believer, even a young child who has faith to be baptized, should be encouraged to be baptized: "...*According to your faith, let it be to you* (Matt. 9:29 NKJV). It should be noted, however, that a child should never be pressured into water baptism; he or she must desire it and be ready for it.

BE BAPTIZED IN WATER

If you have never been baptized in water, what are you waiting for? Do it today. We mentioned earlier that when Jesus hung on the cross between two thieves, one of them was saved, but there was no opportunity for him to come down from the cross and be baptized.

However, you and I have that opportunity. Although baptism does not save us, let's be obedient to the Word of God and take the opportunity to show that we are dead to sin and alive to Christ. If you have any doubts about your baptism in water, I encourage you to be rebaptized. Doubts can cloud your faith and cast a shadow of condemnation on your life. Romans 14:23 says that "...*everything that does not come from faith is sin.*"

It's important that you are living and walking in faith. If you're not sure, be baptized in water so that you can be certain and so that the enemy cannot sow seeds of doubts in your mind. Water baptism is a physical act which reminds you of your faith and freedom in Jesus. You can point to it if the devil tries to lie to you and put doubt in your heart. You can say with assurance, "I was baptized in water, and I know that I'm free. The old man, the former sinful nature, is cut off and has no power over me. Jesus Christ lives strong in my life." Talk to a pastor or small group leader to arrange for your water baptism.

I believe that any believer in Christ can baptize another believer in water. You do not necessarily have to be a pastor or elder to perform a baptism. Paul the apostle often left water baptism to other believers in the Church. He did it simply because they could serve this way. Paul knew that his primary calling was to preach the Gospel and to train others:

> *I am thankful that I did not baptize any of you except Crispus and Gaius....For Christ did not send me to baptize, but to preach the gospel...*(1 Corinthians 1:14,17).

To summarize, water baptism is a sign of an inner cleansing of the heart. It is a public declaration that I have turned from sin to serve Jesus Christ as Lord. It shows that I am dead to sin and alive to Christ. It is a type of New Testament circumcision in which the power of my old nature has been cut off. And most important of all, baptism in water is important because the Lord, in His Word, commands me to be baptized, and I want to be obedient to Him.

ENDNOTE

1. *The New Testament Greek Lexicon*, s.v. "Baptizo," www.studylight. org/lex/grk/view.cgi?number=907 (accessed 24 Sept 2008).

BAPTISM IN WATER
REFLECTION QUESTIONS

1. Name the four types of baptisms mentioned in the Bible. How many of the four have you experienced?

2. If you have been water baptized, what does it mean to you, to Jesus, and to your friends?

3. What is the spiritual explanation of going under and coming back up out of the water? Can you truly say that your "old self" is dead?

4. What brings a clear conscience toward God?

Chapter 10

MORE BAPTISMS

BAPTISM INTO THE BODY OF CHRIST

Baptism into the Body of Christ is another kind of baptism mentioned in the New Testament. We learned earlier that the word *baptize* literally means "to put into." When we're baptized in water, someone places us into the water. When we're baptized into the Body of Christ, the Holy Spirit supernaturally places us into the "Body" or "the family of God":

> *For we were all baptized by one Spirit into one body—whether Jews or Greeks, slave or free—and we were all given the one Spirit to drink* (1 Corinthians 12:13).

We are united by one Spirit as members of the Body of Christ. God gives us other people in the Body of Christ for support and encouragement. As we learn from each other and get to know Jesus better, we are made complete by His Spirit. Jesus is the head of the Body, and each believer makes up a part of His spiritual Body on earth. We are here on earth to become Christ's hands, feet, tongue, and other parts of the Body with various functions, abilities, and callings.

When a young man is newly married, he leaves his old family and is placed into a new family. As a new husband, he, with his wife, starts a new unit of their own. Likewise, a new believer is supernaturally placed in the new family of God to begin life anew. Being baptized into the Body of Christ is a supernatural work of God. We are placed spiritually into the Body of Christ the moment that we receive Jesus Christ as Lord. Because we belong to Christ, we are members and belong to each other.

GOD'S WONDERFUL FAMILY

When you are born again into God's family, you become a brother or sister in Christ to every other believer in the world. Being a part of the Lord's family is a wonderful blessing. You can meet a Christian brother or sister for the very first time from another nation, and it seems like you have known them forever. You are a part of the same family.

Years ago, I visited one of the largest churches in the world in Seoul, Korea. It was a beautiful experience meeting dozens of Korean believers, and although we did not speak the same language, we were able to sense that we were a part of the same spiritual family.

When John, the apostle, saw the throne of Heaven in Revelation 5:8-9, he saw *"living creatures and...elders"* (representing followers of Christ or the Church in all nations and among all kinds of people), giving honor to Jesus: *"And they sang a new song: 'You are worthy to take the scroll and to open its seals, because you were slain, and with your blood you purchased men for God from every tribe and language and people and nation.'"*

God's wonderful family is made up of people from every nationality, race, and culture. We are all brothers and sisters through faith in our Lord Jesus Christ.

The Lord's family is awesome. Each of us has been born again by the Spirit of God. We are sons and daughters of the King of the universe, according to Second Corinthians 6:18:

"I will be a Father to you, and you will be My sons and daughters," says the Lord Almighty.

BAPTISM OF FIRE

Yet another kind of baptism mentioned in the New Testament is the *baptism of fire.* John the Baptist mentions this baptism in Luke 3:16:

John answered them all, "I baptize you with water. But one more powerful than I will come, the thongs of whose sandals I am not worthy to untie. He will baptize you with the Holy Spirit and with fire."

We learned earlier that the baptism with water signifies repentance. Here we see that the coming of the Holy Spirit is proof of the presence of God. Fire is a biblical symbol of purification and power. John the Baptist said that Jesus will baptize us with the Holy Spirit and fire.

Let's talk about the baptism of fire first, specifically in the way that it can purify us. Trials or difficult times that we go through are a type of baptism of fire. After John says that Jesus will baptize us with the Holy Spirit and fire, he explains it more fully in the next verse:

His winnowing fork is in His hand to clear His threshing floor and to gather the wheat into His barn, but He will burn up the chaff with unquenchable fire (Luke 3:17).

A fan or winnowing shovel was used to throw grain into the air so that the chaff would blow away, while the clean kernels fell back to the threshing floor. The Lord tells us that He will clean out His threshing floor, gather the wheat into His barn, and burn the chaff. In other words, our God is committed to cleaning out of our lives all of those unwholesome things (chaff) that may still be clinging to us. This could be habits from our past or old ways of thinking that are contrary to God's Word.

This cleaning process is not always easy, and Christians should not be shocked when they have to face trials in their lives. I grew up on a farm, so I clearly understand the importance of the chaff being separated from the wheat in order to get a clean product. When wheat harvest came each year, we had a large vibrating screen that the wheat was poured onto which literally shook the chaff free as it was separated from the wheat. God is looking for good fruit (wheat) in our lives. Sometimes He allows us to be in circumstances to "vibrate" us a bit until the "chaff" in our lives can be blown away.

On the family farm, I also learned a similar lesson while welding. I remember taking a torch and heating metal until it was very hot. When it was hot, the impurities came to the top. We called it *slag*. When the slag surfaced, we would scrape it off. Otherwise it could keep the two pieces of metal from being properly welded together. Again, this is a picture of a separation of the good from the bad so that we can find purity.

There are times when we need the *slag* skimmed out of our lives in a baptism of fire. When we go through these fiery trials and hard times, the impurities will come to the surface. The wrong attitudes, those things that irritate us, the critical spirit, lack of love, lack of joy, lack of patience, fear—all "come to the top." When the "spiritual slag" is revealed in our lives, we can receive from Jesus the ability to repent and get rid of the impurities.

DRINKING THE CUP

James and John, two of the disciples, had some *chaff* or *slag* in their lives that needed to be eradicated so that they could become stronger. They sincerely loved Jesus and wanted to be close to Him, but they seemed to be focusing mainly on the benefits that Jesus could give them when they sent their mother to ask a favor of Jesus on their behalf (see Matt. 20:20). When their mother asked if her sons could sit on the right and left side of Jesus in His Kingdom, Jesus asked the following hard question:

"...Are you able to drink the cup that I am about to drink, and be baptized with the baptism that I am baptized with?" They said to Him, "We are able." So He said to them, "You will indeed drink My cup, and be baptized with the baptism that I am baptized with..." (Matthew 20:22-23 NKJV).

Were they willing to be baptized with the baptism that He was to be baptized with—namely, to go to the cross? Were they willing to suffer in order to build the Kingdom? Were they willing to face the impurities in their lives and allow Jesus to change them? They thought they were ready, so they said, "We are able." However, a few days later, they deserted their Master when He was arrested (see Matt. 26:56). The benefits of following Jesus just became less desirable to them when it involved suffering for Him!

Of course, the disciples later returned to Jesus after they had betrayed and abandoned Him. They witnessed His love and forgiveness in their lives. Jesus knows and understands our weaknesses. When the impurities come out of our lives, He reaches out with forgiveness and love. His power strengthens us so that we can be victorious the next time that we are faced with life's difficulties.

COUNT IT ALL JOY

You may say, "Lord, I'm having some hard times! Why me?" It is never easy when God allows us to go through the fire. It can make us feel like giving up when God doesn't make sense to us. What God really wants us to do is to keep trusting Him. This is why James 1:2-5 tells us,

> *Consider it pure joy, my brothers, whenever you face trials of many kinds, because you know that the testing of your faith develops perseverance. Perseverance must finish its work so that you may be mature and complete, not lacking anything. If any of you lacks wisdom, he should ask God, who gives generously to all without finding fault, and it will be given to him.*

When we understand that the trials of life can be used by the Lord to work His character in our lives, it really changes our perspective. We can rejoice, because the Lord is using it for our good. And He promises to give us wisdom right in the middle of the trials if we just ask Him. He can be trusted, in spite of the pain.

In high school, I took a course learning how to make certain metal tools. In order for the tools to be hardened, we were taught to take a hot molten piece of metal and dip it in and out of water in order to temper it. This process gave the tool the proper strength to be useful.

Our Lord allows us to go through the baptism of fire in order to make us useful in His service. An attitude of pride will not hold up under pressure. When we go through some fiery trials in life, we learn to trust in the Lord and in His Word. His character is built into our lives. Without His character built into our lives, we will break under pressure when the Lord really begins to use us.

PERSEVERING IN OUR TRIALS

Yes, the Lord will use us, even when we are going through hard times! For example, did you ever have a Brother or Sister "Sandpaper" in your life—someone who rubbed you the wrong way? Maybe the Lord allowed this person in your life for a reason. Perhaps He wanted to see if you would respond in a Christ-like way. So you reached out to the Lord for His strength to love this person unconditionally. It was not easy, and life was unpleasant for awhile, but you came through this baptism of fire with a new love and awareness of God's grace and mercy. Today you have a great relationship with this former "Sister Sandpaper." Trusting Him and persevering really made you strong and cleaned out some bad attitudes in your own life.

Did you ever accidentally pinch your finger, causing a painful blood clot to form under the fingernail? You probably had to go to the doctor, where he used a sterile needle to drill a little hole in the nail to release the pressure. The Lord wants us to release spiritual pressure in the lives of others. But, He can only use us effectively if our attitudes are pure and we trust Him.

When we persevere in our trials, we are purified by the Word of God so that we can be the pure Bride of Christ. The Bible calls the Church "the Bride of Christ." Did you ever see a dirty bride? I haven't. The Lord is cleaning us up. The Book of Ephesians 5:25-27 says,

Husbands, love your wives, just as Christ loved the church and gave Himself up for her to make her holy, cleansing her by the washing with water through the word, and to present her to Himself as a radiant church, without stain or wrinkle or any other blemish, but holy and blameless.

The Lord uses His Word to wash us. However, if we never look into the mirror, we tend to forget how dirty we can be. The Word of God is our mirror and our cleanser. As a little boy, I hated to take baths. But my parents made sure that I took a regular bath, whether I liked it or not! And now, I'm glad they did. You too will look back later and really appreciate your "spiritual bath."

Don't be afraid of the baptism of fire. Jesus will give you the strength to persevere. Trials can make you strong, depending on how you respond to them.

ON FIRE FOR JESUS

Previously we said that fire is a symbol of purification and power, and we have examined how we can be purified by "fiery" trials. Another side to the baptism of fire is the *power* aspect of it. We should live in such a way that our lives are "on fire for Jesus Christ." We need to be earnest and enthusiastic in our love for God, according to Revelation 3:19:

...turn from your indifference and become enthusiastic about the things of God (TLB).

If we are not enthusiastic about the things of God, we are commanded to turn from our indifference or apathy. We have been created to experience His "fire" burning inside of us, baptized with fire. The early disciples "burned" with a zeal for God. Ask the Lord to baptize you with His fire and His zeal. God is looking for zealous men and women. Numbers 25:11-13 speaks of such a zealous man:

Phinehas son of Eleazar, the son of Aaron, the priest, has turned My anger away from the Israelites; for he was as zealous as I am for My honor among them, so that in my zeal I did not put an end to them. Therefore tell him I am making My covenant of peace with him. He and his descendants will have a covenant of a lasting priesthood, because he was zealous for the honor of his God and made atonement for the Israelites.

The Lord honored Phinehas because he was zealous for his God. Are you zealous for your God today? Are you experiencing this type of *baptism of fire*?

Those who are baptized with fire are men and women of prayer who have a holy hatred for sin and a holy love for the Lord with a compassion for the lost and the Church of Jesus Christ. The psalmist in Psalm 69:9 reveals his righteous zeal for God's house and Kingdom: "*...zeal for Your house consumes me....*" When we are truly on fire for God, all the desires of our body and soul are wrapped up in His desires. We are absorbed in who God wants us to be and what He wants us to do. We will have a godly zeal to see His house (His Church) be all that it was created to be in our generation. "Lord, baptize us in your fire!"

MORE BAPTISMS
REFLECTION QUESTIONS

1. Think about a time when you experienced kinship with a believer from a different culture. What did you have in common?

2. What is some "chaff" in your life that God is cleaning away?

3. Can you see how God is molding you through the baptism of fire to become the person that He needs for the task that He wants you to accomplish?

4. Have you seen spiritual growth in your life after coming through a trial? How did God's Word help you?

Chapter 11

BAPTISM IN THE HOLY SPIRIT (PART 1)

THE PROMISE OF THE HOLY SPIRIT

So far, we have covered three baptisms: baptism in water, baptism into the Body of Christ, and baptism of fire. In this chapter and the next, we will look at the *baptism in the Holy Spirit*. It is important to realize how the Holy Spirit desires to use us and flow from our lives. The subject of the baptism in the Holy Spirit is sometimes a controversial one in today's Christian Church, so let's carefully look at this experience to help us understand it better.

Let's look again at Luke 3:16:

John answered them all, "I baptize you with water. But one more powerful than I will come, the thongs of whose sandals I am not worthy to untie. He will baptize you with the Holy Spirit and with fire."

When we previously mentioned this verse, we covered the *baptism of fire* part of it. Now we want to look at what John the Baptist meant when he said that Jesus would baptize us *with the Holy Spirit*.

All genuine believers have the Spirit of God dwelling in them. First Corinthians 3:16 says, *"Don't you know that you yourselves*

133

are God's temple and that God's Spirit lives in you?" The Holy Spirit lives within each child of God. The Holy Spirit is a person, not a doctrine or merely an influence or power. This is very important. The Holy Spirit is God and has the personal characteristics of God. God is the Father, Son, and Holy Spirit—often referred to as the Trinity. The Holy Spirit is the third person of the Trinity.

The divine person of the Holy Spirit comes to dwell in you when you give your life to Jesus and receive Him into your life. He cares about you and has the power to help you. However, this does not mean you have been *baptized* in the Holy Spirit.

HOLY SPIRIT LIVES WITHIN EVERY BELIEVER

At the time of our salvation, the Holy Spirit comes to live within us. He leads and motivates us to live holy lives and delivers us from the bondage of sin. Romans 8:9 says,

You, however, are controlled not by the sinful nature but by the Spirit, if the Spirit of God lives in you. And if anyone does not have the Spirit of Christ, he does not belong to Christ.

During Jesus' last talk with His disciples before His trial and crucifixion, He promised them that they would receive the Holy Spirit (see John 14:16-17). Subsequently, after His resurrection, Jesus visited the disciples and breathed on them, saying, *"Receive the Holy Spirit"* (John 20:22).

At that moment, the disciples were born again by the Holy Spirit. Although the disciples had already confessed Jesus as Lord and were saved according to the old covenant provisions, they could not have been born again before Jesus was raised from the dead. Jesus had to come and give them His resurrection power according to the new covenant. Now they also believed that Jesus was raised from the dead, and their salvation was completed.

When God took a hunk of clay in the Garden of Eden and breathed on it, Adam was formed and received physical life. Here, God breathed on the disciples and gave them spiritual life. When you were convicted of your sin before you received Christ, the Holy Spirit was outside of you bringing conviction. When you received Jesus, the Holy Spirit then came *inside* to live within you. But there's more. The New Testament depicts *two* distinct yet complementary aspects of receiving the Holy Spirit—the experience of the disciples receiving the Holy Spirit on "Resurrection Sunday" that we just described, and the experience they later received on "Pentecost Sunday." Let's compare the two experiences in the next section.

YOU SHALL RECEIVE POWER

After the disciples' encounter with the Holy Spirit when Jesus breathed on them and told them to "receive the Holy Spirit," He made it clear that their experience was still incomplete. In His final words to them before His ascension, He commanded them not to go out and preach immediately, but to go back to Jerusalem and wait there until they were baptized in the Holy Spirit and thus given the power they needed to be effective witnesses:

Do not leave Jerusalem, but wait for the gift My Father promised, which you have heard Me speak about. For John baptized with water, but in a few days you will be baptized with the Holy Spirit...you will receive power when the Holy Spirit comes on you; and you will be My witnesses in Jerusalem, and in all Judea and Samaria, and to the ends of the earth (Acts 1:4-5,8).

The disciples prayed and waited. During the festival of Pentecost, 120 of His disciples were gathered together in one place, and it happened:

> *When the day of Pentecost came, they were all together in one place. Suddenly a sound like the blowing of a violent wind came from heaven and filled the whole house where they were sitting. They saw what seemed to be tongues of fire that separated and came to rest on each of them. All of them were filled with the Holy Spirit and began to speak in other tongues as the Spirit enabled them (Acts 2:1-4).*

Here, the disciples experienced the mighty baptism in the Holy Spirit. Although they had received the life of the Holy Spirit only a few weeks before when Jesus breathed on them (see John 20:22), this time they received the *baptism* in the Holy Spirit. They received a new dimension of the Holy Spirit's power.

This distinction between receiving the Holy Spirit at rebirth and receiving the *baptism in the Holy Spirit* is significant. We need to recognize the difference between having the Holy Spirit living within us and being baptized in the Holy Spirit. The baptism in the Holy Spirit is the Lord's provision for releasing the power of the Holy Spirit into the believer's life.

The story is told of a Christian man who lived in a poor village in the interior of his nation who had the opportunity to come to a big city. Having never experienced the use of electricity before, he was fascinated when he saw electric light bulbs for the first time. He asked his host if he could have one to take back to his home. When he got back to his village, he hung the light bulb on a string in his hut. He was frustrated because it wouldn't work until a missionary explained to him that it must be plugged into a power source. That's the way it is with us. To enter into the fullness of what God has planned for our lives, we have no greater need than to be plugged into the power source. We need the mighty baptism in the Holy Spirit. It is the gateway into a new dimension of the Spirit's presence and power in our lives, and it empowers us for ministry.

WE RECEIVE BY FAITH

Just like salvation comes by faith, so the baptism in the Holy Spirit comes by faith. We receive the baptism in the Holy Spirit by faith in the Word of God and by faith in Jesus Christ. Faith is always a prerequisite for receiving the baptism in the Holy Spirit. Galatians 3:14 tells us explicitly, "*...that by faith we might receive the promise of the Spirit.*"

Not everyone's experience will be the same. We can pray and receive the Holy Spirit baptism on our own or have someone pray for us to receive the power of the Spirit. Some believers have a dynamic, emotional experience at the time of their Holy Spirit baptism. They may begin to sing a new song that God gave to them in an unknown language or speak in tongues. Others simply take God at His Word and experience the reality of the baptism in the Holy Spirit as a process over the days and weeks that follow.

The *type* of experience that we have is not of primary importance; the key is that we *know by faith* in the Word of God that we've been filled and baptized with the Holy Spirit. We need to *know* that we are baptized with the Spirit just as we need to *know* that we have been born again.

It is possible to be baptized in water and in the Holy Spirit at the same time. Or, some may be baptized in the Holy Spirit before they are water baptized. It happened in Acts 10:44-46. Peter was preaching the Gospel to the Gentiles in Cornelius's home when an amazing phenomenon occurred:

> *While Peter was still speaking these words, the Holy Spirit came on all who heard the message. The circumcised believers who had come with Peter were astonished that the gift of the Holy Spirit had been poured out even on the Gentiles. For they heard them speaking in tongues and praising God.*

The people at Cornelius' house received the Word and were saved. The Lord immediately poured out the Holy Spirit on them in power, thus paralleling the disciples' experience at Pentecost. The Holy Spirit baptism brings the personal boldness and power of the Spirit into our lives that we need to be effective.

Regardless of our personal experience, the baptism in the Holy Spirit is received by faith. A pastor and his wife came to me and said, "We're not sure we've been baptized in the Holy Spirit." I assured them they can know for sure as I laid my hands on them and prayed. This time, they chose to "receive the promise of the Spirit through faith," and they were gloriously baptized with the Holy Spirit. From that time on, they knew it. Their spiritual thirst led them to yield to and receive the baptism in the Holy Spirit.

EFFECTIVENESS IS YOUR DECISION

Some might ask, "Do I really have to be baptized in the Holy Spirit?"

My reply would be, "Do you really need to have all of God's power so that you can help other people find God?" People all around us are going to hell. We *need* God's power so that He can fulfill His purpose in us and through us.

I often explain the power of the Holy Spirit like this. If you mow a lawn, you can do it with a scissors or with a lawn mower. It's your decision. You don't have to be baptized in the Holy Spirit to be a Christian, but, like using the mower, it makes you much more effective. In fact, the early disciples of Jesus made being filled with the Holy Spirit a requirement for anyone who was to be set apart for special responsibilities in the Church:

> *Brothers, choose seven men from among you who are known to be full of the Spirit and wisdom. We will turn this responsibility over to them* (Acts 6:3).

The baptism in the Holy Spirit increases the effectiveness of a Christian's witness because of a strengthening relationship with the Father, Son, and Holy Spirit that comes from being filled with the Spirit. The Holy Spirit makes the personal presence of Jesus more real to us, and it results in our desire to love and obey Him more.

SAUL'S EXPERIENCES

Saul was a devout Jew who was playing havoc with the Christians in the Book of Acts. He was on his way to Damascus to persecute the early Christians when the Lord met him and did something supernatural in his life.

> *"Who are you, Lord?" Saul asked. "I am Jesus, whom you are persecuting," He replied. "Now get up and go into the city, and you will be told what you must do."...Then Ananias went to the house and entered it. Placing his hands on Saul, he said, "Brother Saul, the Lord—Jesus, who appeared to you*

on the road as you were coming here—has sent me so that you may see again and be filled with the Holy Spirit" (Acts 9:5-6,17).

Ananias called Saul "brother" because Saul was now a Christian. However, Saul still wasn't filled with the Holy Spirit. Many people say that when you're saved, you are also automatically baptized in the Spirit. Although it is possible to receive and be baptized in the Holy Spirit at conversion, it is not always so. Saul, who became Paul, was baptized in the Holy Spirit three days after he received Christ into his life. It happened when Ananias laid his hands on Saul and prayed.

The difference between receiving the Holy Spirit at salvation and being baptized in the Holy Spirit can be explained like this: You can be led to a pool of water and drink from it (receive the Holy Spirit at salvation), or you can jump fully into the water (be baptized with the Holy Spirit). It's the same water (Holy Spirit), but you have a completely different experience.

During the late 1800s, evangelist Dwight L. Moody was preaching and saw the same two ladies sitting in the front row night after night. Nearly every night, they came up to him after his meetings and said, "Mr. Moody, you need to be filled with the Holy Spirit." At first he resisted their remarks. However, months later, as he walked down a street in New York City, he had an experience with God and was filled with the Holy Spirit.[2]

The results were amazing! He preached the same sermons, but instead of two or three people giving their lives to Jesus at his services, hundreds and thousands came to know Jesus. In his lifetime, a million people were said to have been kept out of hell because of the power of God on his life.[3] What made the difference? The mighty baptism—infilling—of the Holy Spirit. He had received power.

EXPERIENCING HIS POWER

I was baptized in the Holy Spirit seven years after I received Jesus Christ as my Lord. I could have been baptized in the Holy Spirit sooner, but I was ignorant of the Holy Spirit's work. Although I loved the Lord and was part of a youth ministry, I realized that there was something missing in my life. I needed the power of the Holy Spirit. I sometimes attended Christian ministries where people were set free from drugs or other life-controlling problems, and I realized that these people had a spiritual power that I didn't have.

After studying the Scripture and being convinced that this experience was based on the Word of God, I went out into the woods one day and prayed, "God, I want You to baptize me in the Holy Spirit." I prayed, but nothing happened. In retrospect, I can see that I had pride in my heart. I wanted to receive the baptism in the Holy Spirit alone, on my own terms. I didn't really want anything too radical to happen! So, I humbled myself and went to a pastor who laid his hands on me and prayed for me. That night I received the baptism of the Holy Spirit.

After I was baptized in the Holy Spirit, my life immediately took on a whole new dimension of power. It wasn't me—it was God—the baptism in the Holy Spirit gave me an intense desire to please Him. Before I was baptized in the Holy Spirit, I was involved in a ministry where a few people had given their lives to the Lord. However, after I was baptized in the Holy Spirit, everything seemed to change. Hundreds of young people gave their lives to Christ during the next few years. I knew that it certainly wasn't anything that I was doing in my own power and strength. It was the Holy Spirit's power.

I must admit that, at first, I was not sure if I should share this experience with others because it was so controversial in the Church at that time. I changed my mind when a young lady reprimanded me by saying, "Why didn't you tell me about the baptism in the Holy Spirit? Last Saturday night I was baptized with the Holy Spirit, and now I have experienced His power in my life." If you filled a kerosene lantern with oil, you would still have to strike a match and light the lantern so that its power could be released. The same principle applies to the truth of the Holy Spirit. We can have the Holy Spirit living in us but lack the power that He can release in our lives. God spoke to me through this young lady, and from that time on, I told people the truth that I had discovered. It was a joy to serve as a "spiritual midwife" when Jesus baptized them in His precious Holy Spirit.

Although it took me *several* years from the time that I was saved to the time that I was baptized in the Holy Spirit, I believe it is God's will that we are born again and immediately receive the baptism in the Holy Spirit and the power of God in our lives. Acts 2:38-39 says that the baptism in the Holy Spirit was not just for those at Pentecost, but for all who would believe in Christ throughout this age: "*...and you will receive the gift of the Holy Spirit. The promise is for you and your children and for all who are far off....*"

ENDNOTES

1. For more about the baptism in the Holy Spirit, read my booklet, *How Can I Be Filled With the Holy Spirit?* (Lititz, PA: House to House Publications, 2007); www.h2hp.com.

2. R.A. Torrey, "Why God Used D. L. Moody," *Christian Biography Resources*, www.wholesomewords.org/biography/biomoody6.html (accessed 24 Sept 2008).

3. "Dwight Lyman (D.L.) Moody," *Faith Hall of Fame*, www.eaec.org/faithhallfame/dlmoody.htm (accessed 24 Sept 2008).

BAPTISM IN THE HOLY SPIRIT (PART 1)
REFLECTION QUESTIONS

1. Have you experienced the power of the Holy Spirit? Describe your experience.

2. Describe a time when you have experienced a greater effectiveness because of the baptism in the Holy Spirit.

3. Explain the difference between receiving the Holy Spirit and being baptized in the Holy Spirit. Why do you think every person's experience is a bit different?

4. The baptism in the Holy Spirit is for whom?

Chapter 12

BAPTISM IN THE HOLY SPIRIT (PART 2)

RECEIVE GOD'S GOOD GIFT

Some sincere believers have told me they have heard negative things about Spirit-baptized people. So have I. But, we live by the Word of God, not by other people's experiences. We may see something happen in the name of the Holy Spirit that may not be the Holy Spirit at all and think, "If that's the Holy Spirit, I want nothing to do with it." But we cannot throw out the baptism of the Holy Spirit because of what we saw or experienced that was not authentic.

Others may say, "If I'm supposed to be filled with the Holy Spirit, well, that's up to God…I'm open to whatever the Lord wants to do." This sounds like a noble response, but in reality, it may be a statement of unbelief because they do not really want to be filled. A young man told me once that he felt that he did not deserve to be baptized with the Holy Spirit. I told him, "You're right. I don't deserve it either. We don't deserve salvation or anything else, but God wants to give it to us as a free gift."

God has already initiated His part in our receiving Christ and being baptized with the Holy Spirit. It's now up to us to receive by faith what He has freely offered. To be baptized with the Holy Spirit is a personal act of faith, a decision that we make. Our heavenly Father wants to give us the gift of the Holy Spirit:

If you then, though you are evil, know how to give good gifts to your children, how much more will your Father in heaven give the Holy Spirit to those who ask Him (Luke 11:13).

Have you been baptized in the Holy Spirit? If you are not sure, ask! Jesus wants to baptize you with the Holy Spirit. You only need to ask Him in faith, in the same way that a child would ask his father for a gift.

Your heavenly Father wants you to receive the Holy Spirit, and He offers the baptism in the Holy Spirit to you freely! Suppose I gave you a Christmas gift and you took it home, opened it, and found many gifts wrapped up inside. One of these gifts was a tool that you needed, pliers. But you had to take the pliers out and use it in order for it to be effective. The same principle applies to the Spirit of God. We need to receive the gift of the baptism in the Holy Spirit by faith and then begin to use all of the wonderful individual spiritual gifts that accompany it.

WHAT ABOUT TONGUES?

In Ephesus, some of the believers had never even heard of the Holy Spirit. So Paul instructed them, telling how they could receive the Holy Spirit. When he prayed for them, the Holy Spirit came upon them and they spoke with "tongues," sometimes called "spiritual languages":

When Paul placed his hands on them, the Holy Spirit came on them, and they spoke in tongues... (Acts 19:6).

146

There are nine supernatural gifts of the Holy Spirit listed in First Corinthians 12:7-10. The gift we want to look at in this chapter is the gift of tongues:

> *Now to each one the manifestation of the Spirit is given for the common good. To one there is given through the Spirit the message of wisdom, to another the message of knowledge by means of the same Spirit, to another faith by the same Spirit, to another gifts of healing by that one Spirit, to another miraculous powers, to another prophecy, to another distinguishing between spirits, to another speaking in different kinds of tongues, and to still another the interpretation of tongues.*

Often, when believers are baptized in the Holy Spirit, they begin to speak in *tongues* or a new heavenly language. The Bible says that they magnify God (see Acts 10:46). This personal prayer language is understood by God because it is my spirit speaking to God. Speaking in tongues is a direct line of communication between me and God.

In the Book of Acts, speaking in tongues was often the initial outward sign accompanying the baptism in the Holy Spirit (see Acts 2:4;10:45-46;19:6). Should every Spirit-filled believer speak with tongues, then? No, you don't have to, but you may! It's like going into a shoe store and getting a pair of shoes and saying, "Must I have tongues in my shoes?" No! But you can take the tongues because they are part of the shoes. Praying in tongues is a blessing from God. Let's imagine that you came to my home and I gave you a meal. You say, "Must I eat this steak?" or "Must I eat this salad?" Well, no, you don't have to, but it is available for you as part of the whole meal deal.

God wants us to have and use spiritual gifts so that we may be a blessing to others. We need to exercise them so that they can be used in our lives to build us up spiritually and to give us supernatural strength and ability to be effective in our Christian lives. First Corinthians 14:1 says, "*...eagerly desire spiritual gifts....*"

And Jude 20 tells us to "*...build yourselves up in your most holy faith and pray in the Holy Spirit.*"

God wants us to build ourselves up in faith so that we may be powerful witnesses for Christ. In Acts 1:8, we read that, when the Holy Spirit comes upon us, we will receive power to be His witnesses. That's why we receive power—to be His witnesses. Praying in tongues builds us up spiritually. It's like charging your spiritual battery. You can, with power, pray for the sick and minister to people as you continue to build yourself up spiritually by praying in other tongues.

I WISH YOU ALL SPOKE IN TONGUES

Speaking in tongues has been controversial in some parts of the Church of Jesus Christ. One of the first times that I went to a public meeting where I was told that some of the people spoke in tongues, I sat near the back of the building. I wanted to make a quick exit if I became too uncomfortable! Although some believers hesitate because they have heard of or seen misuses of the gift of tongues or other gifts of the Spirit, we have no need to be afraid.

It seems funny to recall now, but one of the fears that I had when I was considering being baptized in the Holy Spirit was that I would be in a place like a department store and the Spirit of God would come on me. I was afraid I'd begin to speak in tongues uncontrollably. I pictured myself being so embarrassed! Then one day I read this Scripture: *"The spirits of prophets are subject to the control of prophets"* (1 Cor. 14:32).

Your spirit is subject to you. It's like a water spigot. You turn it off and on. The water is always there, but it's under your control. You choose to pray or not to pray in tongues at any given time, but it's God who gives you the gift and the power to speak.

How important then is it for us as Christians to speak in tongues and to exercise other spiritual gifts? Paul the apostle wished that every person spoke in tongues and stressed that the gift of tongues was an important part of his spiritual life:

I would like every one of you to speak in tongues....I thank God that I speak in tongues more than all of you (1 Corinthians 14:5a;14:18).

Is someone a second-rate Christian if they don't speak in tongues? No, of course not! But God wants us to be blessed and to use these blessings so that we can fulfill His call on our lives. Some say that they believe it is selfish to pray in tongues. Is it selfish to pray? Is it selfish to read the Bible? Why do we pray and read the Scriptures and speak in tongues? We do it to communicate with God and in order to be built up spiritually so that we can be effective in helping other people.

BYPASSING THE DEVIL

We pray two ways—with our mind and with our spirit. Both are needed, and both are under the influence of the Holy Spirit, according to First Corinthians 14:14-15:

For if I pray in a tongue, my spirit prays, but my mind is unfruitful. So what shall I do? I will pray with my spirit, but

I will also pray with my mind; I will sing with my spirit, but I will also sing with my mind.

The first way that we pray is with our mind. When we pray, "Our Father in Heaven..." it's coming from our mind. We understand it. We are using our intellect to pray in a learned language.

The second way that we pray is with our spirit. When we pray with our spirit (in tongues), it's unfruitful to our mind. Our spirit is praying directly to the Father without having to accept the limitations of our human intellect.

In other words, when you and I pray with our spirit, we have no idea what we are saying, but our heavenly Father knows what we're saying. We come in simple faith and trust God to provide the form of the words and their meaning to Him. Using our new language, we edify ourselves (see 1 Cor. 14:4) or "build ourselves up" spiritually. It is like a direct phone line to God.

I walked into a hardware store one night soon after I was baptized in the Holy Spirit, and there were two men conversing in Pennsylvania Dutch, a language that many people of German descent use in my community. I cannot understand this language at all. Even though I didn't understand, those men understood one another clearly. The Spirit of God spoke to me and said, "In the same way that these two men understand one another, I understand exactly what you are saying when you pray in tongues. Continue to praise Me and magnify Me in this new language that I've given to you." I was set free to pray in tongues from that day on without the nagging thoughts of unbelief and doubt from the devil.

Today, I pray in tongues daily because, when I pray in tongues, I bypass the devil. He has no idea what I'm saying. I'm speaking the "language of angels" and "mysteries" according to God's Word:

...I speak with the tongues of men and of angels... (1 Corinthians 13:1).

For anyone who speaks in a tongue does not speak to men but to God. Indeed, no one understands him; he utters mysteries with his spirit (1 Corinthians 14:2).

KINDS OF TONGUES

To clarify some common misconceptions of tongues, let's look at two different kinds of tongues mentioned in God's Word. The kind of tongues we have mentioned so far is for personal prayer and intercession. This is the type of tongues that magnifies God and is a direct line of communication between us and God. It is God speaking through us.

In the same way, the Spirit helps us in our weakness. We do not know what we ought to pray for, but the Spirit Himself intercedes for us with groans that words cannot express. And He who searches our hearts knows the mind of the Spirit, because the Spirit intercedes for the saints in accordance with God's will (Romans 8:26-27).

P.C. Nelson, founder of the Southwestern Bible Institute, was a Greek scholar. He told his young ministers that the Greek literally reads, "The Holy Spirit maketh intercession for us with groanings which cannot be uttered in articulate speech" (articulate speech is the ordinary kind of speech). He pointed out that the Greek bears out that this not only includes "groanings" in prayer, but also "other tongues."[1] The Bible tells us that the Holy Spirit helps us to pray. Many times I have felt unable to put into words the desires of my heart when I pray. And sometimes situations are so complex that I just do not know how to pray. But the Holy Spirit does!

The second type of tongues is mentioned in First Corinthians 12:28-30, after God says that He has appointed some in the Church for various tasks and responsibilities:

> *And in the church God has appointed first of all apostles, second prophets, third teachers, then workers of miracles, also those having gifts of healing, those able to help others, those with gifts of administration, and those speaking in different kinds of tongues. Are all apostles? Are all prophets? Are all teachers? Do all work miracles? Do all have gifts of healing? Do all speak in tongues? Do all interpret?*

Because this Scripture states, "Do all speak in tongues?" many think this means that not all can speak in tongues as a personal prayer language. However, this Scripture is really asking, "Are all appointed to speak with the gift of tongues *to the Church?*"

You see, there is a gift to be used *in the Church* which is a type of speaking in tongues. It is different from the type of speaking in tongues that we experience when we pray in our prayer language. When this gift of tongues is used in the Church, someone who has the gift gives a message in tongues, and then someone with the *gift of interpretation* gives the meaning, thus building up the Body of Christ.

To summarize, although all Christians may speak in tongues so that we can be built up spiritually to serve God better, He also sometimes gives a special gift of tongues to be used to build up His Church. These Scriptures are clear that not all will be used by God to speak in tongues in a Church meeting. However, we can still pray in tongues as a personal prayer language to the Lord. The same goes for the other gifts listed here. You and I may not have the gift of administration in the Church, but we all must administer our checkbooks. We may not have the gift of healing, but we are all called to pray for the sick in our own families.

EAGERLY DESIRE

After Paul lists the ministry gifts of the Holy Spirit to the Church in First Corinthians 12:28-30, he says in verse 31,

But eagerly desire the greater gifts. And now I will show you the most excellent way.

What is the greater gift? The greater gift depends on the situation you're in. If you need healing, you believe God for the "greater" gift of healing because that is what you need.

What is the "most excellent way?" It is love. First Corinthians, chapter 13, tells us all about it! Some say that they don't need all of these gifts; they just need love. That's not what Paul was trying to communicate. He is emphasizing that possessing spiritual gifts without love amounts to nothing. We need to use these gifts in love, according to First Corinthians 13:8-13:

Love never fails. But where there are...tongues, they will be stilled...For we know in part and we prophesy in part, but when perfection comes, the imperfect disappears. When I was a child, I talked like a child, I thought like a child, I reasoned like a child. When I became a man, I put childish ways behind me. Now we see but a poor reflection as in a mirror; then we shall see face to face. Now I know in part; then I shall know fully, even as I am fully known. And now these three remain: faith, hope and love. But the greatest of these is love.

This passage of Scripture reveals that tongues will cease when *"that which is perfect is come"* (1 Cor. 13:10 NKJV). Some people believe that this means that tongues are no longer needed today. They believe that "that which is perfect" refers to the Bible. However, they fail to realize that the same passage says we shall see *"face to face."* We will not see the Bible face to face. We will see Jesus face to face. At that time, at the end of the age, there will be no need for the gift of tongues. But until we see Jesus face to face, the Lord has given us the gifts of tongues and prophecy and other supernatural gifts of the Holy Spirit to use for His glory here on earth.

CONTINUE TO BE FILLED

Do you know for sure that you are baptized with the Holy Spirit? Do you pray in tongues? Are the spiritual gifts becoming evident in your life? If you are not sure, ask Jesus to fill you with His precious Holy Spirit today. Ask another Spirit-filled believer to pray for you. Sometimes it takes someone else to agree with us in faith to experience the Holy Spirit's filling. Paul went to Ananias. The Samaritans waited for Peter and John. I went to a pastor friend.

We must reach out and receive the promise of the Spirit by faith. By faith we receive, and then are continually filled, day by day. Dwight L. Moody, the famous evangelist, used to say, "I need to be filled with the Holy Spirit every day, because I leak!"[2]

The early believers knew this too, according to Acts 4:31: *"After they prayed, the place where they were meeting was shaken. And they were all filled with the Holy Spirit and spoke the word of God boldly."* Many of these believers were already filled with the Holy Spirit at Pentecost in Acts chapter 2. But they needed to be filled again. We too must experience constant renewal. Paul warns the believers that to maintain the fullness of the Spirit, they must live lives separate from sin:

*Do not get drunk on wine, which leads to debauchery.
Instead, be filled with the Spirit (Ephesians 5:18).*

The New Testament baptism in the Holy Spirit happens in the context of committed discipleship to Jesus Christ. Our hearts must be right with God so that He can pour out His Spirit on us. As we live in obedience to Christ, there will be a greater awareness and presence of the Holy Spirit in our lives. We will deepen our relationship with the Father and grow in our love for others.

God wants to use you to see change come into people's lives. But it takes the Holy Spirit's power to break through. As a Spirit-filled believer, you may have loved ones who have not received Christ. Each person needs to have their own personal experience with God as Savior and Lord and as the baptizer with the Holy Spirit. As the old saying goes, "You can lead a horse to the water, but you cannot make him drink." However, if you place salt on his oats, the horse will become thirsty and drink more quickly. The baptism in the Holy Spirit at work in our lives makes those around us thirsty for living water!

The Lord wants to use you to touch others' lives for eternity. People in your family will be changed when you are baptized in the Holy Spirit. It won't be through your natural ability but through Christ who is at work in you through the Holy Spirit.

Soon after I was baptized in the Holy Spirit, my wife LaVerne asked me to pray for her, and she received the baptism in the Holy Spirit. One by one, many of our extended family members were baptized in the Holy Spirit. Each of our four children, by the grace of God, has been baptized with the Holy Spirit.

God bless you as you live by the power and the authority of God and experience the Holy Spirit flowing through your life.

ENDNOTES

1. P.C. Nelson, quoted in Kenneth E. Hagin, *Seven Vital Steps To Receiving the Holy Spirit* (Tulsa, OK: Faith Library Publications, 1980), 10.

2. Dwight L. Moody, quoted in Joel Comiskey, "The Filling of the Holy Spirit," *CBN.com*, www.cbn.com/spirituallife/BibleStudyAndTheology/Discipleship/Comiskey_SpiritFilling.aspx (accessed 25 Sept 2008).

BAPTISM IN THE HOLY SPIRIT (PART 2) REFLECTION QUESTIONS

1. Gifts must be accepted, opened, and used in order for us to really experience them. How do we accept the gift of tongues that God offers to His children?

2. How can the gift of tongues help you to pray? Do you know what you are saying when you pray in tongues? Does the devil know what you are saying?

3. Can you have and use your prayer tongue even if you do not use it publicly? What is the purpose of tongues when the Church meets together?

4. Why did the believers in Acts 4:31 have to be filled with the Holy Spirit again? Is there evidence of power in your life that you have been baptized in the Holy Spirit?

PART IV

Building for Eternity

Chapter 13

IMPARTING BLESSING
AND HEALING

THE LAYING ON OF HANDS

A few years ago, I visited a Bible School where I met an elderly gentleman. He had experienced God moving in miraculous ways during his lifetime, and I asked him if he would be willing to come to my dormitory room to pray for me. I knew that he had something that I needed. As he laid his hands on me and prayed, I sensed the Lord giving me His blessing through this precious man of God. I knew that, according to the Scriptures, something happens when one believer lays his hands on another believer and prays for him. He *gives* or *imparts* something that goes beyond His teaching or influence, something that the other person needs.

In Leviticus 16:21-22, Aaron laid his hands on a live goat and confessed the people's sins, which were then imparted from his hands to the goat. This supernatural transference happened through the laying on of hands.

What happens in this supernatural transference? The Bible tells us that there is a clear impartation of power and God's blessing that is transferred from one person to another through the laying on of hands. "The laying on of hands" is another one of the important foundation stones that we need to place in our Christian lives from Hebrews 6:1-2:

Therefore, leaving the discussion of the elementary principles of Christ, let us go on to perfection, not laying again the foundation of...laying on of hands... (NKJV).

The Lord's purpose for the foundation stone of *the laying on of hands* is for us to experience the Lord's blessing and to be a blessing to others. In the Old Testament, the laying on of hands was an accepted practice for imparting blessing to be transmitted to future generations. Jacob imparted the blessing of God to his children by laying hands on them before he died (see Gen. 48:14).

A friend of mine tells the true story of a Christian man who realized that he was nearing the end of his life and was soon going to be with his Father in Heaven. He gathered his children around and imparted God's blessings to each of them. He then went into his bedroom, lay down, and went home to be with the Lord. This is a true, modern-day example of imparting the blessing of God.

We don't have to wait until we come to the end of our lives to impart our blessing through the laying on of hands, however! In the next two chapters, we will examine how *the laying on of hands* is for imparting not only blessing, but also healing, spiritual gifts, and authority.

IMPART LIFE TO ONE ANOTHER

There is a tremendous power in our lives to bless, encourage, and help people just by touching them. I believe this especially applies to children. Those who serve in a children's nursery are able to bless children by holding them in their arms and speaking God's Word over them. One night there was a child in our home who continued to cry. I took the crying child in my arms and prayed in the Spirit as I imparted the blessing of God to him. After a few minutes, the child became peaceful. What a privilege it was to impart a spiritual blessing of peace to that child. Jesus Himself did this: *"And He took the children in His arms, put His hands on them and blessed them"* (Mark 10:16). I lay my hands on my children each night before they go to bed. As I pray for them, I am imparting the Lord's health, healing, grace, and anointing into their lives. Why? Because there is power released as we impart spiritual blessings to others.

I love to shake people's hands for the first time. I personally believe that, as a believer in Jesus Christ, we can shake someone's hand and impart, through a type of laying on of hands, faith, conviction, the grace of God, and the Lord's anointing into their lives. The Lord wants us to be a blessing to others so that we may inherit a blessing from Him, according to First Peter 3:8-9:

Finally, all of you, live in harmony with one another; be sympathetic, love as brothers, be compassionate and humble. Do not repay evil with evil or insult with insult, but with blessing, because to this you were called so that you may inherit a blessing.

Something supernatural happens when we understand the principle of the laying on of hands and participate in this life-giving truth. When Spirit-filled Christians lay their hands on others and pray a prayer of faith, the power of God that is in them will also be received by the person for whom they are praying. Did you ever hug someone who had strong perfume on, and then for the next few minutes, you continue to smell that perfume or cologne? In the same way, when someone lays their hands on you, they impart to you something that the Lord has given them. Something that is on them gets on you. We can lay our hands on others and impart the blessings of God to them, and they can do the same for us.

IMPART THE POWER OF THE HOLY SPIRIT

In both the Old and New Testaments, there are numerous examples of the laying on of hands, where one person laid hands on another person for a very specific purpose. Let's take a few moments and look at some distinct purposes that we see in the Scriptures for the laying on of hands.

Notice first of all how the power of the Holy Spirit is imparted through the laying on of hands. In Acts 8:14-15,17, we observe that the laying on of hands helped those who were seeking the baptism in the Holy Spirit:

> *When the apostles in Jerusalem heard that Samaria had accepted the word of God, they sent Peter and John to them. When they arrived, they prayed for them that they might receive the Holy Spirit...Then Peter and John placed their hands on them, and they received the Holy Spirit.*

Peter and John went down to Samaria and laid hands on the new believers, and they received the baptism in the Holy Spirit. You may ask, "Must I have someone lay hands on me to be baptized with the Holy Spirit?" No, you don't have to. However, something supernatural happens when a Spirit-filled believer in Jesus Christ lays hands on another person and prays a prayer of faith. God supernaturally works through His people and gives them the divine ability to impart the mighty power of the Holy Spirit as they pray in faith.

Many years ago, a friend laid his hands on me and prayed, and I began to pray in a new language. (I spoke in tongues.) Now I have the same privilege of laying hands on people and seeing them baptized with the Holy Spirit and praying in tongues. And so do you. The laying on of hands to impart the baptism in the Holy Spirit is not just for the believers in the Book of Acts; it is also true for us today.

Jesus Christ is the same yesterday, today, and forever (see Heb. 13:8). He desires to use you to pray for others to be baptized in the Holy Spirit as you lay your hands on them and pray a prayer of faith. Expect the Lord to use you.

IMPART SPIRITUAL GIFTS

Another purpose for the laying on of hands is for the imparting of spiritual gifts. Paul said in Romans 1:11-12 that he wanted to impart spiritual gifts to the Romans so that they would be strengthened in their faith: *"I long to see you so that I may impart to you some spiritual gift to make you strong—that is, that you and I may be mutually encouraged by each other's faith."*

Jesus wants us not only to impart the baptism in the Holy Spirit through the laying on of hands, but also to impart spiritual gifts that the Holy Spirit gives. First Corinthians 12:8-10 speaks of nine of these supernatural spiritual gifts.

To one there is given through the Spirit the message of wisdom, to another the message of knowledge by means of the same Spirit, to another faith by the same Spirit, to another gifts of healing by that one Spirit, to another miraculous powers, to another prophecy, to another distinguishing

163

between spirits, to another speaking in different kinds of tongues, and to still another the interpretation of tongues.

As we receive particular spiritual gifts from the Lord and learn how to use and exercise them, we can then lay hands on others and impart these gifts to them. These are not the only gifts that the Holy Spirit gives to the Body of Christ to be used among His people. Other gifts mentioned in Romans 12:6-8 are the gifts of prophecy, serving, teaching, encouraging, giving, leading, and mercy. These gifts are inward desires or motivations that we have that enable us to build up God's people and to express His love to others.

There are many supernatural and very practical spiritual gifts that God gives us. When God gives them to us, He then gives us the power and ability to lay our hands on others so they also can see these gifts begin to blossom in their own lives. The Lord wants to use you to impart to others what He has given you.

Maybe you need *discernment* or a *gift of faith*. Find someone who has this gift operating in his or her life. Ask him or her to lay hands on you and pray for you. Many times I have asked others to lay their hands on me and pray for me, and I have received supernatural ability and spiritual strength. Other times, I have had the privilege of laying my hands on others and imparting a gift of faith, and they received spiritual strength and a renewed faith.

RECEIVING IMPARTATION

The anointing and gifts of God are enhanced by associating with people who have these kinds of gifts operating in their lives. This gives us a greater opportunity to get these gifts transferred or imparted to us. When we rub shoulders with those who have certain spiritual gifts, they can lay their hands on us to impart that gift to us. In First Timothy 4:14, Paul said, "*Do not neglect your gift, which was given you through a prophetic message when the body of elders laid their hands on you.*"

The leaders of the Church laid their hands on Timothy, and God gave him the spiritual gifts that he needed to fulfill his responsibilities. Paul told Timothy not to neglect the gifts that he had received from the Lord through the laying on of hands. He also told Timothy that he needed to stir up these gifts:

> *For this reason I remind you to fan into flame the gift of God, which is in you through the laying on of my hands* (2 Timothy 1:6).

If you have the gift of prophecy or the gift of serving or the gift of mercy, you can stir up these gifts as you pray in the Spirit and exercise these gifts. As you confess the truth of the Word of God and thank God that He has given you these gifts, you stir them up within you so that you can be a blessing to those around you.

IMPART HEALTH TO THE SICK

The laying on of hands is also associated with the ministry of physical healing. The Lord wants us to be open to His Spirit's prompting, to pray for others, and to have others pray for us to see God's healing power released. The Bible tells us in Mark 16:17-18 that "*...these signs will accompany those who believe: In My name...they will place their hands on sick people, and they will get well.*"

This promise is for every believer. The Scriptures tell us that those who believe in Jesus will lay their hands on the sick, and they will recover. God has called you and your family to lay hands on those who are sick. For many Christians, the first thing they will do when someone is sick is to call the doctor or go to the drugstore. The first thing we should do when someone is sick is to lay our hands on that person and pray. God tells us that they will recover. The healing power of God goes from one believer to another through the laying on of our hands. There's nothing wrong with going to the doctor, but we need to go to Jesus first.

We read in the Book of Acts, chapter 9, that Ananias, who understood the power that is released through the laying on of hands and prayer, laid hands on Saul for healing:

> ...*Placing his hands on Saul, he said, "Brother Saul, the Lord—Jesus, who appeared to you on the road as you were coming here—has sent me so that you may see again and be filled with the Holy Spirit." Immediately, something like scales fell from Saul's eyes, and he could see again...* (Acts 9:17-18).

Saul had given his life to Jesus Christ on the road to Damascus. Three days later, Ananias prayed for Saul, and two things happened. First of all, Saul had been blind for three days, and there were scales on his eyes. The Scripture says the scales fell from his eyes when Ananias laid his hands on him and prayed for him. Secondly, Saul was filled with the Holy Spirit.

Jesus constantly imparted health to others as He touched them. We see it in Mark 1:41-42 when Jesus healed a man with leprosy: "*Filled with compassion, Jesus reached out His hand and touched the man....Immediately the leprosy left him and he was cured.*"

We again see Jesus' healing impartation in Mark 6:56:

166

And wherever He went—into villages, towns or country-side—they placed the sick in the marketplaces. They begged Him to let them touch even the edge of his cloak, and all who touched Him were healed.

Jesus lives in each of us today. As we take a step of faith and believe God's Word, we will also be vessels of healing. When we lay our hands on the sick and pray a prayer of faith, the Bible says that they will recover.

ANY BELIEVER CAN IMPART

The laying on of hands is not just for leaders to practice. Every believer can transmit spiritual blessings to others in this way. As God's people, we are the Church. When we read the New Testament, we do not see the Church as a group of believers who only met together in a building on a Sunday morning; they had interactive relationships with each other daily. They were an integral part of each others' lives:

Every day they continued to meet together in the temple courts. They broke bread in their homes and ate together with glad and sincere hearts, praising God and enjoying the favor of all the people. And the Lord added to their number daily those who were being saved (Acts 2:46-47).

These believers were experiencing true church. They knew how to impart God's blessing to each other as they related closely together as God's people. The same thing is happening all over the world today. People are getting excited about their relationship with Jesus Christ. People are tired of dead religion. They want the real thing. When Jesus Christ saves them and baptizes them in the Holy Spirit, these believers do not want to just sit around and "play church." They want relationships—with Jesus and with each other. They open up their homes and minister to people right in their own homes.

Small, interactive groups that meet together from house to house and also in larger meetings to receive teaching and experience times of worship are popping up all over the place—cell groups, house churches, fellowship groups, small groups—no matter what you call them, they have the purpose of raising mature Christians and giving every Christian a job to do. Small groups give everyone an opportunity to bless others and to impart their lives to others. In small spiritual family groups, the next generation of believers can be nurtured and blessed.

There are times when I feel like I am totally depleted of faith. Since faith comes by hearing the Word of God (see Rom. 10:17), I know that meditating on God's Word is the first step to experiencing renewed faith. But many times I have also been renewed in faith when someone who is "full of faith" prays for me, imparting faith and the healing power of Jesus to me. God has made us in such a way that we need each other. We are His Body, and each part of the Body is important. When we have a need, the Lord often chooses to use others to impart into our lives what we need. The Lord also wants to use us to impart into others' lives what He has given to us.

IMPARTING BLESSING AND HEALING
REFLECTION QUESTIONS

1. What is supernatural about the laying on of hands? Have you ever asked another Christian to impart a blessing to you by the laying on of hands? Describe what you asked for.

2. List the nine spiritual gifts found in First Corinthians 12. List seven more spiritual gifts found in Romans 12. Do you have any of these gifts? Have you imparted any of them to others?

3. Explain in your own words, "anointing comes by association." According to Second Timothy 1:6, how can you stir up the gifts that God has given you?

4. Give some examples of ways that the Lord may want to use you to impart spiritual blessings to others.

Chapter 14

IMPARTING AUTHORITY

ACKNOWLEDGING A SPECIFIC MINISTRY

Another purpose for the laying on of hands is to publicly acknowledge that someone has received authority from God for a specific ministry and to send them out to fulfill it. Acts 13:2-3 gives an account of the spiritual leaders at the church in Antioch acknowledging and sending out two apostles by laying hands on them:

> *While they were worshiping the Lord and fasting, the Holy Spirit said, "Set apart for me Barnabas and Saul for the work to which I have called them." So after they had fasted and prayed, they placed their hands on them and sent them off.*

The church leadership imparted to Barnabas and Saul, through the laying on of hands, the blessing and the grace that the Holy Spirit had given them. They were commissioned for a specific ministry, which acknowledged the call of God already on their lives. Barnabas and Saul were sent out as one of the most powerful missionary teams that ever walked on the face of the earth.

In Acts, chapter 6, a group of men were set apart to distribute food to the widows and to those who were needy. These men were brought before the apostles, who laid their hands on them and imparted to them authority and responsibility for the specific work of food distribution. Because of their history of godliness and faithfulness to the Lord, these "deacons" were set apart for ministry in serving the Church in this way:

They chose Stephen, a man full of faith and of the Holy Spirit; also Philip, Procorus, Nicanor, Timon, Parmenas, and Nicolas from Antioch, a convert to Judaism. They presented these men to the apostles, who prayed and laid their hands on them (Acts 6:5-6).

The Scriptures teach us that those who have received authority from God (they already have a proven ministry) should be set apart or consecrated for this specific ministry in the Church by the laying on of hands by their church leaders. When I was a young pastor, the spiritual leaders to whom I was accountable laid their hands on me and appointed me to a new role of leadership. The Lord used them to establish this new leadership appointment in my life.

AN OLD TESTAMENT EXAMPLE

An Old Testament example of the laying on of hands for authority in a specific ministry is mentioned in the story of Moses and Joshua. Moses faithfully led the children of Israel in the wilderness. When he came near the end of his ministry, he asked the Lord to appoint a new leader over Israel who would take his place. Joshua, whom Moses had trained for 40 years, took his place in leadership among God's people. Let's see what happened during that time of transfer of leadership. We can see clearly the principle of the laying on of hands in Numbers 27:18,20:

So the Lord said to Moses, "Take Joshua son of Nun, a man in whom is the spirit, and lay your hand on him....Give him some of your authority..."

This happened, of course, when Moses realized the need for Joshua to become the next leader. Joshua already was trained by Moses and called by God, but Moses acknowledged his call by laying hands on Joshua and imparting some of the power and authority that the Lord had given him to lead God's people. Joshua was filled with the spirit of wisdom after Moses imparted his authority to him (see Deut. 34:9). Moses imparted to Joshua the spiritual ability and blessing that he had received from the Lord.

SPIRITUAL LEADERS IMPART AUTHORITY

The Bible teaches us that the spiritual leaders whom the Lord places in our lives have been given godly authority and responsibility for us. The Lord commands them to watch out for our souls. Hebrews 13:17 tells us,

Obey your leaders and submit to their authority. They keep watch over you as men who must give an account. Obey them so that their work will be a joy, not a burden, for that would be of no advantage to you.

First of all, in the Body of Christ, we have God's authority because we are sons and daughters of the Lord through faith in Jesus Christ. But as we become involved in the Church in areas of ministry, we not only receive authority from God directly, but we also receive authority as we are commissioned by the spiritual leaders whom the Lord has placed in our lives.

In whatever area of service we find ourselves, we would be wise to ask these questions: "Lord, have you placed one or more spiritual leaders in my life who are watching out for me?" "Lord, is there someone with whom I can share some of my responsibility?" When the timing is right, the Lord may ask us to lay our hands on someone else to impart the blessings and spiritual gifts that the Lord has given to us.

When I was sent out of our local church with a team of leaders to begin a new church nearly 30 years ago, I asked our church leadership to pray for us to send us out with their blessing. I submitted myself to two pastors who laid their hands on me and prayed. These two spiritual leaders saved me and our leadership team from many pitfalls in spiritual leadership as I served as a new pastor.

Spiritual leaders should lay their hands on new pastors, leaders, and missionaries, commissioning them to new areas of service. Hands are laid on them to impart the spiritual blessings and gifts that God gives. Something supernatural happens when we lay hands on others and set them apart for a particular ministry. Those who lay their hands on new Christian leaders are responsible to the Lord to "watch out for the souls" of those they are commissioning.

During the past 20 years, I have had the privilege of laying my hands on and praying for many new spiritual leaders who started churches throughout the world as I mentored them in spiritual leadership.

DON'T BE HASTY

A few years ago, I read about a major revival in southeast Asia where a young man came to know Jesus, and God started to use him in a mighty way. The elders of the Church came together, laid their hands on him, and prayed, giving him authority and responsibility to be sent out as an evangelist. Nearly everywhere he went, people were saved and healed. The Church started to grow, and miraculous things happened. After a while, this young man got puffed up with pride and eventually fell into immorality.

When the leaders of the Church lovingly confronted him, the young man said, "Look, miracles and healings are happening; who are you to tell me what to do?" He was not willing to be accountable for his actions and refused to repent of his sins. The same leaders, who had laid their hands on this young man a few years earlier, commissioning him into this work, informed the young man that they felt responsible.

"Here's what we're going to do," they told him. "We care about you as a person, but we believe that your disobedience to the Lord has caused you to misuse the power of God. We are going to pray and receive back that anointing, that empowering that we gave you when we laid hands on you." Do you know what happened? After they had their time of prayer for "decommissioning," the young man no longer received the power of God to heal the sick, and the miracles stopped happening. From that day on, the evangelist did not see the kinds of miracles that he was accustomed to experiencing.[1] The leaders of the Church realized that they had laid hands on this young leader, giving him responsibility and authority as an evangelist, too soon. They learned the hard way what the Scripture warns us about in First Timothy 5:22: "*Do not be hasty in the laying on of hands....*"

Church leaders need to be careful not to lay hands on new elders, pastors, and ministry leaders prematurely. A person set apart for ministry must have a history of faithfulness to the Lord.

When spiritual leaders lay hands on someone, they stand as God's representatives and give that person authority in Christian service. There is spiritual power released through the laying on of hands when the Lord's people are set apart for specific ministry. In the same way, this authority can be received back.

KEEP YOURSELF PURE

After First Timothy 5:22 mentions that we should not be hasty in laying hands on someone, it continues to say, "...*and do not share in the sins of others. Keep yourself pure.*"

We can "share in" or be a part of another person's sin, if we lay hands on him and he has known sin in his life. This verse may be speaking mainly about commissioning someone in the Church into specific service, but I believe it can relate to any person for whom we pray.

For example, one evening a young lady in our small group asked us to pray for her because she was having severe back problems. Someone discerned that she needed to forgive a family member first. When asked about it, she was quick to say that she could not forgive the person who had hurt her. We encouraged her to first forgive so that she could fully receive the prayer of faith for her healing, which she did. We were then able to pray in faith for her to be healed after she was willing to forgive the person who had wronged her. It is important to first pray with others and to help them find freedom by confessing their sin, repenting of it, and receiving God's Word and forgiveness before we impart God's blessing or authority to them. Only then will the laying on of hands be truly fruitful.

God wants to use you to lay hands on others to impart His blessing and authority. Everywhere you go, God wants to give you opportunities to impart the authority of God to people. We need, of course, to use wisdom in doing it. For instance, men should minister to men, and women to women, as much as possible. The Scriptures seem to imply that older men should be reaching out to younger men and that older women should be reaching out to younger women. Paul gives Titus this guideline,

> *Likewise, teach the older women...then they can train the younger women...Similarly, encourage the young men...* (Titus 2:3-4,6).

If I'm going to impart the blessing or authority of God to a woman, I will have someone else join me for this time of ministry. It's important to use discretion. Proper boundaries should always be maintained between a man and a woman, especially as we lay our hands on them for prayer, so that there are no misunderstandings. The Scripture tells us to "abstain from every form of evil" (1 Thess. 5:22 NKJV).

DELEGATED AUTHORITY

Let's imagine that I go to the bank and take my father's check-book with a check signed by my father. I would have his delegated authority to get money out of the bank. Let's ask the Lord, "How can I impart Your blessing and authority to people today?"

The Scriptures tell us that we are priests. According to First Peter 2:9, we are a royal priesthood:

> *But you are a chosen people, a royal priesthood, a holy nation, a people belonging to God, that you may declare the praises of Him who called you out of darkness into His wonderful light.*

Remember what the priests did in the Old Testament before Jesus came? They stood between the Lord and His people.

Today, in a new way, we are able to take the blessings of God through the laying on of hands and impart them to people, even to people who aren't yet Christians. The Bible says in Second Corinthians 3:6 that we are "ministers of a new covenant." You and I are ministers today and can minister to people through the laying on of hands. When they are sick, we minister healing in Jesus' name. When there is a lack of peace, we minister His peace. When they are weak, we minister His strength. When they need to be filled with the Holy Spirit, we minister the precious Holy Spirit.

If you are a part of a small group of believers in a small group or house church, you know that you can do the "work of ministry." You do not have to wait for your small group leader, pastor, or elder to pray for others—you can do it yourself. There are times when you need to go to the hospital to pray for someone who is sick. At a time like this, you should ask the others in your small group to lay hands on you and pray for you. They will impart God's blessing and anointing into your life so that you can be more effective as you pray for the sick and minister in the name of Jesus Christ at the hospital.

If you are a parent, lay your hands on your children and minister to them. You minister the authority of God, the grace of God, and the anointing of God to your children through the laying on of hands. I have often had the privilege of imparting His peace, His wisdom, and His strength to people. I have also been privileged to have had many people lay their hands on me and impart these same blessings to me. That is what God wants us to do: minister to one another.

RECEIVING AUTHORITY FROM OTHERS

If you are involved in a specific area of ministry, have you ever had someone lay hands on you and commission you into this area of service? Maybe you have a ministry to children in the Church or in the community. Receive the Lord's blessing and authority through the laying on of hands. Ask those whom the Lord has placed in your life as spiritual overseers to lay their hands on you and pray for you. The Scriptures tell us in Hebrews 13:7, *"Remember your leaders, who spoke the word of God to you. Consider the outcome of their way of life and imitate their faith."* Your spiritual leaders have something you need—you can copy their faith and practices because they are strong in the faith. In doing so, you receive an impartation from them.

Perhaps your local pastor or small group leader could lay his or her hands on you and commission you to serve in a particular way. This way you will have God's authority, as well as the authority and blessing of His Church, to do those things that the Lord has called you to do.

ENDNOTE

1. Sutarman Soediman Partonadi, *Sadrach's Community and Its Contextual Roots: A Nineteenth Century Javanese Expression of Christianity* (Rodopi, 1990), 208-209.

IMPARTING AUTHORITY
REFLECTION QUESTIONS

1. Why is it important to receive impartation from leaders before being sent out in a specific ministry?

2. Name some valid reasons for refusing to lay hands on someone.

3. Explain in your own words what "abstaining from an appearance of evil" means in the context of the laying on of hands.

4. Give examples of how you have ministered to others through the laying on of hands.

Chapter 15

WE WILL
LIVE FOREVER

THE RESURRECTION OF THE DEAD

In this chapter, we will examine the important foundation stone of the "resurrection of the dead," and in the next chapter—"eternal judgment."

> *Therefore, leaving the discussion of the elementary principles of Christ, let us go on to perfection, not laying again the foundation of...resurrection of the dead, and of eternal judgment* (Hebrews 6:1-2 NKJV).

Why is the resurrection of the dead so important to our faith? The difference between Christianity and all other religions is that at the very center of Christianity is this truth: Jesus Christ is alive today! Mohammed is dead. Buddha is dead. All these "great prophets," who founded various world religions, are dead, but Jesus Christ is alive! The early Church proclaimed clearly, "Jesus Christ is alive from the dead." It was the foundation of their faith that Jesus Christ had risen from the dead and was alive and well.

The fact of His resurrection is at the center of our faith. He is alive from the dead—this is central to the Gospel of Jesus Christ. Jesus was raised from the dead, and those who believe in Christ will share His resurrection. We will live forever. In fact, at the end of time, everyone will be resurrected, including the wicked, who will be judged and punished. Jesus Himself spoke of the resurrection of the dead, both of the godly and the ungodly, in John 5:28-29:

> *Do not be amazed at this, for a time is coming when all who are in their graves will hear His voice and come out—those who have done good will rise to live, and those who have done evil will rise to be condemned.*

WE WILL LIVE FOREVER

There is an incredible amount of hope that comes from knowing there will be a resurrection of the dead. For one thing, without eternal life, there are no lasting relationships. Since relationship is so important to God, He created us as eternal beings. He wanted to fellowship with us forever. Christians will have relationships (with God and each other) throughout eternity because we will live forever!

When Jesus was walking on this earth, His own brother, James, did not realize that He was the Son of God (see John 7:5) until Jesus arose from the dead and appeared to him. James became an instant believer. Wouldn't you?

> *...Christ died for our sins according to the Scriptures...He was buried...He was raised on the third day according to the Scriptures...Then He appeared to James, then to all the apostles* (1 Corinthians 15:3-4,7).

I have gone to many funerals. For those who are true Christians when they die, there is hope. They go on to be with the Lord. Hope surrounds the entire funeral because the resurrection of the dead assures us that we will see them again in the future.

Those who don't believe in eternal life have no hope of the future resurrection of the dead. Thomas Paine, known widely by his connection with the American and French revolutions, was also a noted infidel who died miserably, in rebellion against the God to whom he turned a deaf ear. When Christians tried to share with him during his last days on this earth, his response was, "Away with you, and your God too! Leave the room instantly!" Among the last utterances that fell upon the ears of the attendants of this dying infidel, and which have been recorded in history, were the words, "My God, My God, why hast thou forsaken me?" He died without hope.

Everyone lives forever because they are eternal beings. Jesus speaks of a resurrection of life for the believer and a resurrection of judgment for the wicked in John 5:24:

> *I tell you the truth, whoever hears My word and believes Him who sent Me has eternal life and will not be condemned; he has crossed over from death to life.*

Christians will live forever with the Lord because they have heard God's Word and believed, but unbelievers will be condemned to live in eternal damnation (hell) forever (see 2 Thess. 1:9).

DEATH IS ABOLISHED

The resurrection of Jesus is a triumph over death. Jesus defeated the devil when He rose from the dead. In First Corinthians 15:25-26, we read that the last enemy to be abolished is death: *"For He must reign until He has put all His enemies under His feet. The last enemy to be destroyed is death."*

I have a book in my home that is filled with hundreds of stories telling what happened in the last moments of peoples' lives before death. Some are wonderful stories about Christians who, during the last moments on this earth, catch a glimpse of Heaven and peacefully go on to be with the Lord.

However, there are horrible stories told of the end for atheists or agnostics or those who cursed the name of God. Nurses in the same room were horrified because these unbelievers were literally seeing the fires of hell before they died.[2]

Friends of ours had their mother living with them for the last years of her life. This elderly Christian woman, who loved the Lord with all of her heart, had cataracts in her eyes for years. The day that she passed away and went on to be with the Lord Jesus, the cataracts fell from her eyes. The blue eyes that she had had in her youth again sparkled. She looked to the corner of her room and reported that she saw Jesus.

While I was in the nation of Zambia, I met a young lady who told an amazing story of Heaven. She had just been in a serious car accident, and while she was unconscious, she saw a bright light coming into the back of the van. She found herself carried away up into the heavenlies where glorious beings were singing in an angelic language. As she got closer to the most beautiful place that she had ever seen, she began to descend back to the earth. She sensed disappointment when she realized that she was not continuing on toward the glorious city that she had seen. The next thing that she saw was the top of the bed rails in a hospital room and the voice of a family member saying, "You'll be OK."

"But I want to go on," she told the angelic being at her side.

"It's not your time yet," the angel responded. Then she awoke on the hospital bed. The Lord had given her a small taste of Heaven!

Christians have incredible hope because of the resurrection of the dead. When Jesus arose from the dead, He abolished death. We are eternal beings who will live forever with Him.

THE BOOK OF LIFE

Did you know that the Lord has every believer's name written in a book called the Book of Life? When we receive Jesus Christ as the Lord of our lives, our names are entered in His book. He will give us the strength to overcome sin and the temptations of this world until the end.

He who overcomes will, like them, be dressed in white. I will never blot out his name from the book of life, but will acknowledge his name before My Father and His angels (Revelation 3:5).

Picture this Book of Life containing a complete record of every person's life on electromagnetic recording tape. Modern technology allows an error to be simply and completely erased in a few moments by running the recording head past that particular stretch of tape a second time. There is even a "bulk eraser" which can, in a few seconds, completely erase the whole recorded contents of an entire tape. So it is with the heavenly record of the sinner's life. When a sinner comes for the first time in repentance and faith to Christ, God applies His heavenly "bulk eraser." The whole record of the sinner's former sins is thereby instantly and completely erased, and a clean tape is made available, upon which a new life of faith and righteousness may be recorded. If at any time thereafter the believer should fall again into sin, he needs only to repent and confess his sin, and God erases that particular section of the record, and once again the tape is clean.

When you stand before God, and Jesus Christ is seated at the right hand of the Father, He will say, "I gave my life for you." Your sins were completely cleansed and taken away two thousand years ago! That is why I love Jesus Christ so much; He paid the price for my salvation on the cross!

WE GRADUATE TO HEAVEN

When you are saved and come to know Jesus, your spirit is saved. When you die and pass on to eternal life, your spirit goes directly into the presence of Christ in Heaven. Immediately, you will be *"absent from the body and...present with the Lord"* (2 Cor. 5:8 NKJV).

When Jesus comes again for His people, both those who have died in Christ and the faithful who are still alive are going to receive new, resurrected bodies adapted for Heaven. Our spirit, soul, and body will come together at that time into a new resurrected body as we live for God throughout eternity. This body will possess an identity with the body of this life and be recognizable (see Luke 16:19-31), will be adapted for Heaven and free from decay and death (see 1 Cor. 15:42), will be powerful and free from disease (see 1 Cor. 15:43), will not be bound by the laws of nature (see Luke 24:31; John 20:19; 1 Cor. 15:44), and will be able to eat and drink (see Luke 14:15; 22:14-18,30; 24:43). So then, for the Christian, death is like graduation. We are passing on from one phase of life to the next phase of life!

Heaven is going to be a wonderful place. Worshiping God in His presence will be the best experience of all. Just think for a moment about the most wonderful things that you enjoy doing on this earth, and then realize that Heaven will be a billion times better than that. Revelation 21:1-4 speaks of Heaven:

> *Then I saw a new heaven and a new earth, for the first heaven and the first earth had passed away, and there was no longer any sea. I saw the Holy City, the new Jerusalem, coming down out of heaven from God, prepared as a bride beautifully dressed for her husband. And I heard a loud voice from the throne saying, "Now the dwelling of God is with men, and He will live with them. They will be His people, and God Himself will be with them and be their God. He will wipe every tear from their eyes. There will be no more death or mourning or crying or pain, for the old order of things has passed away."*

Heaven will be a place of total relief. We'll be totally caught up in the presence of God.

Augustus Toplady, author of the immortal song, "Rock of Ages," was dying at age 38, but he was ready for graduation day. About an hour before he died, he seemed to awaken from a gentle slumber. "Oh, what delights! Who can fathom the joys of the third heaven? What bright sunshine has been spread around me! I have not words to express it. All is light, light, light—the brightness of His glory!"[4]

WHAT ABOUT CHILDREN?

Sometimes people ask, "What about children? Do children go to Heaven? Yes! When children are born into this fallen world, they are born with a fallen nature. However, a young child is not old enough to know the difference between God's laws and the cravings of his fallen nature. When a child comes to the "age of accountability," he has to make the decision to choose right from wrong. He eventually chooses God, or he chooses his own way, which leads to eternal separation from God.

Children are without guilt and spiritual accountability until they sin against God's law. Paul says he was "once alive apart from the law," showing us that a child is "alive" until he understands the difference between right and wrong: *"Once I was alive apart from law; but when the commandment came, sin sprang to life and I died"* (Rom. 7:9). Only God knows when that time is. However, after a child comes to the realization that he is sinning against the law of God, he is spiritually dead. That is why we need to give our lives to Jesus Christ and be born again.

Our four children were convicted of their sins at a young age and received Jesus Christ as their Lord and Savior. When they were babies, they had no understanding of conviction of sin. However, the day came (their "age of accountability") for each of them to respond to the Holy Spirit's conviction.

Every person must come to a place of decision and respond to Jesus Christ and His offer of salvation in order to secure his or her place in Heaven. Jesus said in Matthew 18:3,

> *Assuredly, I say to you, unless you are converted and become as little children, you will by no means enter the kingdom of heaven.*

JESUS IS PREPARING A PLACE

At this very moment, the Lord is preparing a place for us to live throughout all of eternity. Jesus tells us in His Word,

> *Do not let your hearts be troubled. Trust in God; trust also in Me. In My Father's house are many rooms; if it were not*

so, I would have told you. I am going there to prepare a place for you. And if I go and prepare a place for you, I will come back and take you to be with Me that you also may be where I am (John 14:1-3).

Can you imagine it? Jesus is preparing a special place just for you in Heaven! Jesus Christ is coming back for us. Those of us who are still alive on this earth when He returns will meet Him in the air. Those who are dead, whose spirits are with the Lord, will return with the Lord, and He will give them new bodies. It is going to be an exciting day.

Brothers, we do not want you to be ignorant about those who fall asleep, or to grieve like the rest of men, who have no hope. We believe that Jesus died and rose again and so we believe that God will bring with Jesus those who have fallen asleep in Him. According to the Lord's own word, we tell you that we who are still alive, who are left till the coming of the Lord, will certainly not precede those who have fallen asleep. For the Lord Himself will come down from heaven, with a loud command, with the voice of the archangel and with the trumpet call of God, and the dead in Christ will rise first. After that, we who are still alive and are left will be caught up together with them in the clouds to meet the Lord in the air. And so we will be with the Lord forever (1 Thessalonians 4:13-17).

Jesus Christ is coming back for His Church—His people. It is going to be the most historic event since His visit to this planet two thousand years ago. As Christians, we should live each day as if He is coming today. If He doesn't come back for a few years yet, that's OK. We will just keep looking up, expecting His return, as we live in fellowship with the Holy Spirit each day.

D.L. Moody, an evangelist from the 19th century, knew that a place was being prepared for him in Heaven. On his deathbed, he seemed to see beyond the veil as he exclaimed, "Earth recedes, heaven opens before me. It is beautiful. If this is death, it is sweet. There is no valley here. God is calling me, and I must go. This is my triumph; this is my coronation day! I have been looking forward to it for years."[5]

ENDNOTES

1. John Myers, *Voices From the Edge of Eternity* (Uhrichsville, OH: Barbour Publishing, 1994), 133.

2. Myers, *Voices From the Edge of Eternity*.

3. Derek Prince, *Foundation Series* (Lancaster, UK: Sovereign World International, 1986), 579.

4. Myers, 23-24.

5. *Ibid.*

WE WILL LIVE FOREVER
REFLECTION QUESTIONS

1. What fact is central to the Gospel of Jesus Christ? Why is it so important?

2. Are any of your sins recorded in the Book of Life? Why or why not?

3. How is death like a graduation? What do you think Heaven will be like with a new and perfect body, soul, and spirit?

4. When is Jesus coming back for us?

Chapter 16

GOD
JUDGES ALL

ETERNAL JUDGMENT

In the previous chapter, we examined the principle of the "resurrection of the dead." In this chapter, we will look at another basic foundation stone of the Christian faith that is linked to the resurrection of the dead—"eternal judgment."

> *Therefore, leaving the discussion of the elementary principles of Christ, let us go on to perfection, not laying again the foundation of...eternal judgment* (Hebrews 6:1-2 NKJV).

What is judgment? The word *judgment* literally means "a formal decision given by a court"—a verdict.[1] When a judge sentences someone, he passes the verdict. Judgment is pronounced. There is no reversal. The Scripture says that judgment is eternal. Eternal judgment is a verdict given that will last forever.

What is eternity? Imagine one little bird coming to the seashore every one thousand years. This bird then takes one grain of sand and carries it from the seashore and drops it somewhere into the ocean. After all of the sand on all of the seashores along all of the oceans of the world would be totally depleted of sand, eternity would have just begun! It is *that* hard to fathom the length of eternity!

Every man and woman who has ever lived will someday be judged by God for all of eternity: *"Just as man is destined to die once, and after that to face judgment"* (Heb. 9:27). The faithful do not need to fear God's judgment because they will receive eternal life in Heaven with Jesus. The wicked, however, will be eternally punished:

> *Then they will go away to eternal punishment, but the righteous to eternal life* (Matthew 25:46).

Voltaire was a noted French infidel who spent most of his life ridiculing Christianity. When Voltaire had a stroke, which he realized would terminate his life, he was terrified and tortured with such agony that at times he gnashed his teeth in rage against God and man. At other times, he would plead, "O Christ! I must die—abandoned of God and of men!" Voltaire's infidel associates were afraid to approach his bedside. His nurse repeatedly said that, for all the wealth of Europe, she would never want to see another infidel die. It was a scene of horror that lies beyond all exaggeration.[2]

While Heaven is a place of unimaginable beauty where God's people will fellowship with each other and their God forever, hell is a place of endless suffering and punishment for those who reject Christ (see Mark 9:43; Rev. 20:11-15).

THE JUDGMENT SEAT OF CHRIST

Someday we will all stand before the living God in judgment. For believers in Jesus Christ, whose sins were judged on the cross two thousand years ago, it will not be a judgment of condemnation. However, those who have not received the Lord Jesus Christ into their lives will await sentencing. There is no escape.

*For we must all appear before the judgment seat of Christ,
that each one may receive what is due him for the things
done while in the body, whether good or bad. Since, then, we
know what it is to fear the Lord, we try to persuade men...*
(2 Corinthians 5:10-11).

Now is the time to tell people the good news that will set men
and women free. Today, as I write this, I had the privilege of assisting a young couple as they gave their lives to Jesus Christ. Because
of their decision for Christ, their sins are forgiven, and they will not
have to face eternal punishment. They will live forever in God's
Kingdom!

Praise God for Jesus, who paid the price on the cross to save us
from eternal damnation! When we receive Jesus as Lord, He says, "I
love you, I will cleanse you, and I will make you a brand new person as a part of My family. You will live with Me forever." It is God's
plan for us to be saved.

*For God did not send His Son into the world to condemn the
world, but to save the world through Him* (John 3:17).

GIVING AN ACCOUNT

Although believers are free of God's judgment of condemnation
and will go to Heaven, the Bible does say that we will have to give
an account as to the degree of our faithfulness to God, according to
First Corinthians 3:12-15:

*If any man builds on this foundation using gold, silver, costly
stones, wood, hay or straw, his work will be shown for what
it is, because the Day will bring it to light. It will be revealed
with fire, and the fire will test the quality of each man's work.*

If what he has built survives, he will receive his reward. If it is burned up, he will suffer loss; he himself will be saved, but only as one escaping through the flames.

On that Day, at the judgment seat of Christ, God will examine openly our character, secret acts, good deeds, motives, attitudes, etc. If we have not lived holy and godly lives and shown mercy and kindness, our foundation is weak—one of wood, hay, or stubble, rather than of gold, silver, or precious stones. Although we will receive salvation, we will experience great "loss." A careless believer suffers loss in the following ways: loss of dignity (feeling shame) at Christ's coming (see 1 John 2:28), loss of his life's work for God (see 1 Cor. 3:13-15), loss of glory and honor before God (see Rom. 2:7), loss of opportunity for service and authority in Heaven (see Matt. 25:14-30; 5:15; 19:30), and loss of rewards (see 1 Cor. 3:12-14; Phil. 3:14; 2 Tim. 4:8). When our attitude and motivation reflects the fruit of the Spirit and a Christ-like love, our works will be built with precious stones with many rewards from God. If we are motivated more by selfish ambition than by the leading of God's Holy Spirit, those works will be destroyed—burned up. These solemn words should motivate us to live faithful, self-sacrificing lives for the Lord.

A well-known Bible teacher who has spent dozens of years proclaiming the Gospel throughout the world writes the following to describe the moment when God will judge every Christian's works:

In the fiery rays of those eyes, as each one stands before His judgment seat, all that is base, insincere, and valueless in His people's works will be instantly and eternally consumed. Only that which is of true and enduring value will survive, purified, and refined by fire. As we consider this scene of judgment, each of us needs to ask himself: How may I serve

Christin this life, so that my works will stand the test of fire
in that day?[3]

THE JUDGMENT OF THE WICKED

Although everyone, living or dead, throughout the ages will be
judged, the Bible portrays a different picture of the final destiny of
the lost as they stand before the living God. Revelation 20:11-15
says,

*Then I saw a great white throne and Him who was seated on
it. Earth and sky fled from His presence, and there was no
place for them. And I saw the dead, great and small, standing
before the throne, and books were opened. Another book
was opened, which is the book of life. The dead were judged
according to what they had done as recorded in the books.
The sea gave up the dead that were in it, and death and
Hades gave up the dead that were in them, and each person
was judged according to what he had done. Then death and
Hades were thrown into the lake of fire. The lake of fire is the
second death. If anyone's name was not found written in the
book of life, he was thrown into the lake of fire.*

What is the *second death* mentioned here? The *second death* is
an eternal hell that burns with fire for ever and ever. This terrible
picture of hell is almost too horrible to think about, but according
to the Bible, there is a real, burning hell. The Scriptures tell us,

*The Son of Man will send out His angels, and they will weed
out of His kingdom everything that causes sin and all who do
evil. They will throw them into the fiery furnace, where there
will be weeping and gnashing of teeth. Then the righteous*

will shine like the sun in the kingdom of their Father. He who has ears, let him hear (Matthew 13:41-43).

The destinies of both the Christian and the unbeliever are irreversible at death. In Luke 16:19-31, we read the story of the rich man and Lazarus. The rich man spent his life consumed in self-centered living and found himself in hell after he died. Lazarus was a beggar, a poor man who lived in the rich man's neighborhood and was fed by the crumbs that came from the rich man's table. His heart was right with God, and when he died, he was immediately taken to paradise. The rich man cried out because of his torment in hell, but it was too late.

Some people say sarcastically, "I'm not afraid of hell. I'll just be having a party with all my friends." Hell will not be a party. It will be an eternal fire—a place of horrible torment.

FOR THE DEVIL AND HIS ANGELS

Jesus did not make hell for people. He made hell for the devil and his angels:

Then He will say to those on his left, "Depart from me, you who are cursed, into the eternal fire prepared for the devil and his angels" (Matthew 25:41).

The worst thing about hell is the lack of the goodness of God. Everything good that we know of is from God. Can you imagine being in a place where there is nothing good? That is what hell is going to be like, in the midst of all the torment from the fires of hell.

Just like there are degrees of reward in Heaven, there are degrees of punishment in hell, according to the Bible:

That servant who knows his master's will and does not get ready or does not do what his master wants will be beaten with many blows. But the one who does not know and does things deserving punishment will be beaten with few blows. From everyone who has been given much, much will be demanded; and from the one who has been entrusted with much, much more will be asked (Luke 12:47-48).

In other words, those persons who have heard the Gospel and know about the Truth (Jesus) and simply continue to turn away from Him are under a much worse judgment than those who have never heard. I used to think that the people who have been involved in all kinds of "gross sin"—like murder, sexual perversion, and witchcraft—would have the worst punishment in hell. However, here the Bible tells us that people who know the truth and do not obey will have a stricter punishment in hell than those who didn't know or obey. The sobering truth, however, is that hell is hell. Whether it is a million degrees or ten million degrees, it is hell—a *"fire that never goes out"* (Mark 9:43), a place of endless torment and pain, a terrifying reality for those condemned.

THOSE WHO HAVE NEVER HEARD

Jesus Christ is the only way that we can get to God and live eternally with Him. Jesus said in John 14:6, *"I am the way and the truth and the life. No one comes to the Father except through Me."*

So what about people who have never heard of Jesus Christ? We can be assured that God is a fair judge. The Bible says that He is righteous (see 1 John 2:1). When someone questions the fairness of God's judgment concerning those who have not heard, my initial response often is, "But *you* have heard; what is *your* response to Jesus?" Romans 2:14-15 says,

> *Indeed, when Gentiles, who do not have the law, do by nature things required by the law, they are a law for themselves, even though they do not have the law, since they show that the requirements of the law are written on their hearts, their consciences also bearing witness, and their thoughts now accusing, now even defending them.*

Here we see that the Lord judges according to what someone has learned, what his conscience tells him. Everyone has a measure of knowledge of right and wrong, and we need to trust God to be a fair judge. God is a faithful and just God (see 1 John 1:9). He is more just than any human being could ever be. It is those of us who do know the truth of Jesus Christ who have no excuse. Galatians 6:7-8 says,

> *Do not be deceived: God cannot be mocked. A man reaps what he sows. The one who sows to please his sinful nature, from that nature will reap destruction; the one who sows to please the Spirit, from the Spirit will reap eternal life.*

That is why we should sow into our lives spiritually. We must read and meditate on the Word of God and share its truth with others. We need to develop an intimate relationship with our Lord Jesus. Whatever we sow spiritually, we will reap spiritually. Whenever we sow from the flesh (our own evil nature), we will reap that kind of eternal destiny. Let's sow to the Spirit and live for Him throughout all of eternity.

> *But seek first His kingdom and His righteousness, and all these things will be given to you as well* (Matthew 6:33).

What *things*, you ask? All the blessings of God, including eternal life in Heaven. People live forever. What is the Kingdom of God? It is God and His people. It's a relationship with God and relationships with one another that will last forever.

TELL THEM THE GOOD NEWS

Charles Peace was a criminal who was sentenced to death in England. On the morning of his execution, the prison chaplain sleepily read some Bible verses to him. Peace was shocked at his apathetic reading.

He said, "If I believed what you and the church of God say that you believe, even if England were covered with broken glass from coast to coast, I would walk over it, if need be, on hands and knees and think it worthwhile living, just to save one soul from an eternal hell like that'"[4] Christians know that Christianity is real and that an eternal destiny awaits both the saved and the unsaved. That is why we must share the good news.

In the early days of our church, God gave a vision to a young man:

I saw in my vision the fires of hell. And I saw many, many people walking toward the fires, falling over the cliff into hell. Then I saw another group of people, an army. I saw people joining together hand in hand, and they were going down to the brink of the fire and pulling people up at the last moment before they went plunging over. People were being literally snatched from hell. That is what God has called us to do as a church.

We must do whatever we can to see people snatched from the fires of hell to live for God eternally.

When Christians see themselves as spiritual soldiers in His army, we will be motivated to pull people out of the fires of hell because we know the truth that will set them free. The truth will set those free who respond to the name of Jesus.

Many times during flooding or other calamities in our nation, the soldiers from the Coast Guard are brought in to help. They obey the voice of their commander and save the lives of those in danger. As Christians, we are spiritual soldiers. When I travel to various parts to the world, I try to keep my eyes and ears open to my commander, the Holy Spirit, to share my testimony of life in Christ to those whose hearts He has opened. I returned a few days ago from a trip to Africa, and I had the privilege of sharing my testimony of giving my life to Christ with a man from China on the plane.

Jesus Christ is coming back soon. We have a job to do! Jesus admonished believers to remember all of the lost souls who will spend eternity in hell if the Gospel is not presented to them. The fields are ready and white for harvest now, and we must tell them the good news. Jesus said,

> Do you not say, "Four months more and then the harvest"?
> I tell you, open your eyes and look at the fields! They are ripe
> for harvest (John 4:35).

The reality of an eternal judgment should cause all believers to hate sin and diligently seek the lost to tell them of God's wonderful plan for mankind.

People who joke about hell have no idea how real hell will be. After an individual dies, there will be no more opportunity to escape (see Heb. 9:27). There is an old saying, "The road to hell is paved with good intentions." If you have not done so already, now is the time to accept God's provision of His Son, Jesus Christ, for you to live forever! Don't delay.

ENDNOTES

1. Merriam-*Webster's Collegiate Dictionary*, 11th ed., s.v. "Judgment."

2. John Myers, *Voices From the Edge of Eternity* (Uhrichsville, OH: Barbour Publishing, 1994), 22.

3. Derek Prince, *Foundation Series* (Lancaster, UK: Sovereign World International, 1986), 579.

4. Leonard Ravenhill, *Why Revival Tarries* (Grand Rapids, MI: Bethany House, 2004), 32.

GOD JUDGES ALL
REFLECTION QUESTIONS

1. What will be "brought to light" in a believer's life on judgment day, according to First Corinthians 3:12-15?

2. If a person's name is not found in the Book of Life, what is his final destiny, according to Revelation 20:11-15? Is this destiny reversible (see Luke 16:19-31)?

3. How will God be a fair judge, according to Romans 2:14-15?

4. How can you snatch someone from the brink of hell? Have you ever done this?

PART V

Freedom From the Curse

Chapter 17

WHAT
Is a Curse?

SIN CHANGES A PERFECT WORLD

God had a perfect plan for this world. His plan for the human race, starting with Adam and Eve, was that all of creation would be blessed. There would be no sickness, disease, or poverty (see Gen. 1-2). There would be only beauty and health and abundance. However, Adam and Eve disobeyed the commandment that God gave them about the tree of the knowledge of good and evil, and sin entered the world. They trusted in themselves and in their own ability to make a decision that seemed right in their eyes instead of obeying God, and they made a fatal mistake. This mistake has affected all of us:

> Therefore, just as sin entered the world through one man, and death through sin, and in this way death came to all men, because all sinned (Romans 5:12).

Due to Adam and Eve's disobedience to the Lord when they chose to believe the lies of the devil, we now live in a "cursed" or "fallen" world. In the fall of Adam, sin gained entrance into the human race. All humans are now born into the world with an impulse toward sin and evil. Each of us comes into the world with a sinful nature and a natural tendency to go our own selfish way with little concern for God or others (see Rom. 8:5-8).

SATAN CAUSES HAVOC

Because of what Adam and Eve did by breaking the law that God gave them, the ground (nature) was cursed. God told Adam, "...*cursed is the ground because of you; through painful toil you will eat of it all the days of your life*" (Gen. 3:17b). Adam would now have to work with sweat and toil in order to provide for himself, and eventually death would come to him and his offspring.

Sin and its curse began to increase in the world, and the world experienced the "wages" of this sin: "*The wages which sin pays is death*" (Romans 6:23 AMP). This "death" includes all of the heartaches and miseries that come from sin. Sin brings destruction into every area of our human existence.

We can see sin's destruction evidenced in the misery that people experience in today's world—hundreds die from AIDS every week, and hundreds more are infected by this killer virus; a relative or friend may suddenly have a heart attack, and another may die of cancer; brutal gang rape, murder, and violence terrorize countless victims, and so on. There seems to be an upsurge of atrocious crimes being committed daily. Who is responsible for these horrors? If God really cares, some people ask, why are people starving in parts of the world? I believe it all boils down to the fact that we are constantly faced with the power and activity of satan in this world in one way or another. From the beginning of time, he has caused havoc in the world. Satan intends to afflict us with his lies and treachery. Down through the ages, satan and his demons have continued to plague mankind as a result of the initial curse.

In this section of this book, we will take a closer look at all that is involved in the curse and how to be freed from its bondages. Although sin has cursed mankind, Christ provided everything that we need to defeat sin and satan!

JESUS REIGNS OVER THE DEVIL

Satan is the father of sin and the god of this world system. He brought sin into the world, and he tries to entice people into all sorts of evil. He controls this present evil age because the world is in rebellion against God's rule and is enslaved to him (see 2 Cor. 4:4; Luke 13:16; Gal. 1:4; Eph. 6:12; Heb. 2:14). But the glorious, good news is that Jesus came to destroy the works of the devil! He came to dissolve the power, influence, and connection of sin in our lives. The Bible tells us in First John 3:8 that "...*the reason the Son of God appeared was to destroy the devil's work.*"

Jesus has undertaken a holy war against satan, who wants to ruin the work of God in this world. This was Jesus' purpose for coming to the earth two thousand years ago. Jesus' plan is to destroy the works of the devil in our lives. He came to establish God's Kingdom in our hearts and to deliver us from satan's dominion. By His death and resurrection, Christ initiated the defeat of satan, which will eventually culminate in complete and total victory over him at the end of this age. Because of Jesus, we do not have to fear the curse and its effects. Jesus is more powerful than satan! Jesus acknowledges His supreme power over the devil, the ruler of this world, in John 14:30 when He says, "...*the prince of this world is coming. He has no hold on Me.*"

Jesus also says,

You, dear children, are from God and have overcome them, because the one who is in you is greater than the one who is in the world (1 John 4:4).

The Holy Spirit, who lives in every Christian, is greater and more powerful than the devil and his demons, who are in the world. He will fight our battles and give us the victory. We can overcome the devil and his evil schemes in this world because we have been given the victory through Jesus.

JESUS BECAME A CURSE FOR US

We can be completely free from the curse of breaking God's law. We can be free from the devil's lies over our lives because of what Christ did on the cross. The Bible says that He redeemed us from the curse:

Christ redeemed us from the curse of the law by becoming a curse for us, for it is written: "Cursed is everyone who is hung on a tree" (Galatians 3:13).

When the mob called for Jesus to be crucified, they wanted Him identified as a cursed person because, according to Jewish law, anyone who hung on a tree was under God's curse (see Deut. 21:23). So Jesus, on our behalf, was crucified and became a curse for us. He was crowned with a crown of thorns, the very symbol of sin and guilt, because He is the Lamb of God who takes away the sin of the world (see John 1:29). Every curse over our lives was placed on Jesus when He hung on the cross nearly two thousand years ago. We are redeemed and set free of the curse!

The word *redeemed* means "to buy back."[1] I've heard the story of a young boy who, after spending many hours constructing a little boat, took it out on the lake to sail it. With a long string attached to the boat, the boy was having a great time as the boat floated and bobbed. Suddenly, the string tore. In an instant, he lost his prized possession and could only watch as the boat headed downstream where it eventually exited into the river. He thought that it was gone forever.

Several years later, this lad entered a pawn shop in a town downstream from where he grew up. He spotted the boat that he had built years before. The young man approached the storekeeper and said, "This is my boat. My initials are carved on the bottom."

The owner said, "Well, I'm sorry, but somebody brought that boat into my store, and I bought it from him. You'll need to pay me for it." The young man immediately paid the shopkeeper so that he could buy back his cherished boat.

This is a picture of what God did for us. First of all, God made you and me. We went our own way; He redeemed us and bought us back again. By the blood that Jesus shed on the cross two thousand years ago, we have been redeemed (or bought back) from the curse of breaking God's law that was over our lives.

Jesus broke the curse, but we must seek the freedom. The devil can keep the curse over people's lives when they do not know that Jesus has given them authority to break the curse or when they do not walk in the authority of Christ who sets them free.

TURNED OVER TO DARKNESS

If we have been redeemed and set free, why then, along with the rest of mankind, do Christians suffer financial loss, serious illness, emotional upheaval, and other problems? The reasons that people suffer vary greatly. In this section, we are going to take a look at the first of three general reasons why people suffer in this world.

Jesus once healed a man who was blind from birth (see John 9:1-3). The disciples asked Jesus, "Who sinned, this man or his parents, that he was born blind?" (See John 9:1.) Jesus answered that neither the man nor his parents had sinned. Why had he suffered then? It was through no fault of his own that he was born blind. Why do people often find themselves afflicted in some way or another through no apparent fault of their own?

We have to go back to the fact that there is a curse in the world. We learned earlier that sin entered the world through the "curse of the law." The curse of the law is God's label for all the distresses experienced as a result of mankind's initial sin. Since the time when Adam and Eve disobeyed God (broke His law or sinned), *we have lived on a planet that was turned over to the powers of darkness.* Ever since that time, the world has suffered under satan's rule. Believers along with nonbelievers experience suffering as an ongoing consequence of the fall of Adam and Eve. Much of what happens is often simply the result of life in a fallen world. For example, cancer and other diseases may be the result of an unhealthy diet of highly processed foods, foods that have lost their food value due to pesticides, preservatives, and chemicals.

Imagine this scenario. A beautiful garden is given to an evil landlord. What was once filled with beautiful flowers, plants, and food, is soon filled with thistles and thorns. One day a kind and caring man pays a great price and purchases the garden. He gives it back to the former caretakers and gives them clear instructions to make it beautiful and profitable again. Bit by bit, with much hard work, the garden becomes alive. This is what Jesus did for mankind! He paid the great price of His own life in order to purchase back the world. Jesus went to the cross to initiate the defeat of satan and destroy satan's power in our lives. We have been given the authority, as followers of Jesus on this earth, to replace evil with love, health, forgiveness, peace, and blessing for all.

God never intended for wars, disease, cancer, murder, starvation, and poverty to be a part of His plan. God does not cause the evil that happens to us in this world (see James 1:13). However, God is sovereign and allows the evil in the world to happen under His permissive will. At times He will directly intervene, but often He allows bad to happen even though He does not desire it. Evil often continues unabated in this world because the devil continues to operate through individuals who do not serve God and have no power over the devil to resist evil.

God permits evil to continue for the time being. But at the end of the age, satan will experience his final demise when God throws him into the lake of fire forever (see Rev. 20:7-10).

Until that time, says Romans 8:23, believers groan inwardly, because of the effects of living in a sinful world: "*We ourselves, who have the firstfruits of the Spirit, groan inwardly as we wait eagerly for our adoption as sons, the redemption of our bodies.*"

Although we have the Spirit and His blessings, we still groan inwardly because we live in a sinful world and experience its imperfections, pain, and sorrow. We are groaning for the complete redemption that will be given at the resurrection when the glory of God will be revealed (see 2 Cor. 5:4). Until that time, we must walk in God's grace, strength, and comfort, which bring spiritual victory into our lives.

HUMANS MAKE WRONG CHOICES

A second reason why people (both believers and unbelievers) suffer on our planet is simply this: *people make wrong choices.*

God created mankind to have fellowship with Him. He did not create robots who were programmed to make perfect choices. God wants us to fellowship with Him and obey Him because we want to, not because we have to. God made us in His image with the ability to choose. And sometimes our choices are bad. What happens then?

There is a law in this universe set up by God called "the law of sowing and reaping." The Bible says in Galatians 6:7 that "...*a man reaps what he sows.*" In other words, if we make wrong choices in life, we will have to reap the consequences. If we drive recklessly, we will probably have an accident. If we mistreat our bodies, we may have serious health problems. If we refuse to work, we may have to go without food and clothing. The sins of immorality and adultery often result in the breakdown of a marriage.

Wrong choices not only affect an individual, they may affect his family and those around him—and even future generations. An alcoholic father not only ruins his own life, but his life-style also has a devastating effect on his whole family. The Bible says that the sins of parents can follow their children to the third and fourth generations (see Exod. 20:5; Deut. 5:9).

A young man I was counseling once told me that he didn't want to end up like his father. His father's lifestyle and example were deplorable and undesirable. Sometime later, this man chose to turn away from Christ, and the most astonishing thing happened during the next few years. The young man's lifestyle and characteristics became like those of his father. Since this young man was no longer living in obedience to Jesus Christ as his Lord, he was unable to break the curse that was passed down from his father's generation to his generation. In fact, this curse had been passed down to his life from many preceding generations and caused him to continue to live in bondage. This is why Jesus gave His life on the cross. He became a curse for us so that we no longer need to fear reaping what was sown by our ancestors.

As Christians, we must act in accordance with God's Word and avoid whatever will remove us from God's protection. We must confess known sin and examine our lives to see if we are displeasing the Holy Spirit. However, when we do make bad choices, even innocently, God may allow hardships and suffering into our lives as a means of discipline so that we again submit to His will and walk in faith. When God disciplines us, He does so because He loves us, according to Hebrews 12:5-6:

> *My son, do not make light of the Lord's discipline, and do not lose heart when He rebukes you, because the Lord disciplines those He loves, and He punishes everyone He accepts as a son.*

God wants us to live holy lives as His children. Suffering is sometimes a tool that God uses to get our attention. He wants to accomplish His purposes for our lives and to get us to trust Him completely. Sometimes we must endure hardships because they can serve as a catalyst to spiritual growth: "*No discipline seems pleasant at the time, but painful. Later on, however, it produces a harvest of righteousness and peace for those who have been trained by it*" (Heb. 12:11). Suffering forces us to trust in God rather than ourselves.

DIRECT SATANIC ATTACK

Direct satanic attack is a third reason people suffer in this world. The New Testament is filled with people who suffered because demons tormented them, and it continues to happen today.

Demonic curses are sometimes placed on a person so that he or she is crippled emotionally, spiritually, and even physically. The word *curse* means "A prayer or invocation for harm or injury to come upon one."[2] Those involved in satanic cults sometimes attempt to place curses on others. People who have had curses placed on them may have an unexplained accident or go through specific kinds of problems.

Balak, king of the Moabites, tried to place a curse on the Israelites who were coming in his direction. Balak had heard the stories of how the God of the Israelites had destroyed their enemies, and he was scared. So he called a prophet named Balaam and asked him to put a curse on the people of Israel. His plan did not work. The children of Israel had chosen to follow God's plan for their lives, and no enemy could defeat them (see Num. 22).

Believers are not always immune to satan's attacks and bondages. Even though Job was a righteous man who walked with God, the Lord allowed satan to attack him. Paul was a spirit-filled godly man, yet he experienced a "thorn in the flesh" that he described as a messenger of satan. Both men suffered, but God used their afflictions to teach them important spiritual lessons. These men learned to live victoriously because they knew that they ultimately had authority over the power of satan and his demons just as we do today.

Usually direct satanic attack occurs for two reasons:

1. We are not walking under the protection of Christ or fail to walk in His power, therefore opening our lives up to demonic attack.

2. In the case of Paul, he was walking in such a great revelation that Jesus allowed satan access to him so that he would not become proud (see 2 Cor. 12:7).

We must break the power of satan by waging intense spiritual warfare. We live in a spiritual world. The enemy is out to destroy us any way that he can. The devil has come to steal, kill, and destroy (see John 10:10). When satan can attack, he will. As Christians, we must be alert to satan's schemes:

Be self-controlled and alert. Your enemy the devil prowls around like a roaring lion looking for someone to devour. Resist him, standing firm in the faith, because you know that your brothers throughout the world are undergoing the same kind of sufferings. And the God of all grace, who called you to His eternal glory in Christ, after you have suffered a little while, will Himself restore you and make you strong, firm and steadfast (1 Peter 5:8-10).

Although, as Christians, we do not have to walk in fear of satan and his demons, satan is our enemy. We have been delivered from his power, but as a roaring lion, he remains a threat to us and seeks to destroy us. We must stand firm in the faith. No matter what kind of suffering he inflicts or how he tries to influence our emotions, our thoughts, or our actions, God will see us through.

ENDNOTES

1. *Merriam-Webster's Collegiate Dictionary*, 11th ed., s.v. "Redeem."
2. *Ibid.*, s.v. "Curse."

WHAT IS A CURSE?
REFLECTION QUESTIONS

1. Why was the ground cursed in Genesis 3:17? What happened as a result (see Rom. 6:23)?

2. How does Jesus destroy the works of the devil in our lives?

3. How do our choices make a difference in the way that our lives are lived? Is it possible to be affected by the sins of our ancestors?

4. Are believers immune to satan's attacks? How can we be alert to satan's schemes (see 1 Pet. 5:8-10)?

Chapter 18

RECLAIMING WHAT THE ENEMY STOLE

WE CAN BE VICTORIOUS

If we have the power of God living in us and are set free from the curse of the law, then why are some Christians living as if they have not been redeemed and set free? Yes, even as Christians, we may find in ourselves areas of bondage, even though we have given our lives to Jesus Christ and are filled with His Holy Spirit.

First of all, as Christians, we need to realize that *we can have victory in every area of our lives!* (See Romans 8:37.) This victory is promised in the first book of the Bible when God promises to redeem the world, giving us the victory over satan.

The devil is the most cursed being in the entire universe, and his demise is certain (see Rev. 20:10). That's why he wars so relentlessly against God and His people. But his fate was already sealed in the third chapter of Genesis. God tells the serpent that there would be a spiritual conflict between the offspring of the woman (Jesus Christ) and the offspring of the serpent (satan and his demons):

So the Lord God said to the serpent, "Because you have done this, cursed are you above all the livestock and all the wild animals! You will crawl on your belly and you will eat dust all the days of your life. And I will put enmity between you and the woman, and between your offspring and hers; he will crush your head, and you will strike his heel" (Genesis 3:14-15).

God promises that Christ would be born of a woman and be "struck" through His crucifixion. But even though He was struck, He would rise from the dead to completely crush satan, sin, and death. Jesus came to earth to deliver us from satan's dominion and to establish God's Kingdom in our hearts. He came to give us life and victory!

Tragedies are not a part of God's plan for your life—they have not originated in Heaven. The Bible tells us clearly that every good gift comes from above (see James 1:17). One of satan's most subtle schemes is to try to cause us to blame God for the bad things that happen in our lives. We have already discussed that the trials and sufferings in our lives have various causes—because we live in a sinful world, because we make wrong choices, or because of direct satanic attack. If we look at the root of all of these causes, we notice that they have satan at their core! So we can never blame God.

God is the One who provides a way out of our bondage to sin and suffering. He has a plan for our lives that is filled with hope. God can take the most negative circumstances and turn them around for good. No matter how dark our circumstances seem at the moment, we can be full of hope. Jesus helps us to come through every obstacle victoriously. His plans for you are plans of peace and not of evil; He wants to give you a future and a hope (see Jer. 29:11).

Jesus understands suffering because He was willing to suffer more than anyone ever has by taking our sins upon Himself when He died on the cross. There He broke the powers of darkness and provided forgiveness for us, setting us free from the curse.

LIVE IN COVENANT WITH GOD

We must realize, like Abraham did, that we have a covenant with God. In a covenant made with Abraham in Genesis 17:7, God promised,

> *I will establish My covenant as an everlasting covenant between Me and you and your descendants after you for the generations to come, to be your God...*

With this Old Testament covenant, God promises Abraham to bind Himself to His faithful people to be their God. God continued this relationship in the New Testament when He made a new covenant with us in Jesus Christ. The new covenant is a promise to bestow divine protection and blessing on those who, through faith, accept Christ and receive His promises. Galatians 3:6-9 says,

> *Consider Abraham: "He believed God, and it was credited to him as righteousness." Understand, then, that those who believe are children of Abraham. The Scripture foresaw that God would justify the Gentiles by faith, and announced the gospel in advance to Abraham: "All nations will be blessed through you." So those who have faith are blessed along with Abraham, the man of faith.*

All who believe, as Abraham believed, share in Abraham's blessings. We have inherited the blessing of Abraham through faith in Jesus Christ. Faith brings blessing.

Our relationship with God is secured by His blood, but the depth of our fellowship with Him may fluctuate. It depends on our obedience to God. We must maintain a close fellowship with God so that we can be blessed, according to Deuteronomy 28:1-3.

But if we do not heed the voice of the Lord, we will be under a curse (see Deut. 28:15). A curse is the absence of a blessing. Turning away from fellowshipping with God results in a curse on our lives. We cannot expect God to bless us if we have turned away from Him.

Nevertheless, believers are assured that if they love Jesus and depend on Him, He will never leave or forsake them (see Heb. 13:5). He will be their helper through any difficulties. Jesus Christ has come to set us free, to make us whole in every area of life.

It is not the will of God for evil to come upon our lives. It's not God's will for sickness, confusion, depression, fear, insecurity, or inferiority to come upon us. However, as we learned before, we will not always be exempt from suffering. That does not negate the fact that God wants us to be free from all of these afflictions. They are a part of the original curse, and God wants us to be free. He has created us to be whole.

When I was a child, I had a heart murmur. Some of my relatives also had heart problems. I believe it was a product of a curse genetically passed down from generation to generation. When my schoolmates were having fun playing sports, I had to stand on the sidelines and watch. Often, to make matters worse, the teachers recruited me to be the umpire. Every time I had to call a close play, the team that didn't agree with me let me know in no uncertain terms they thought I was a lousy umpire.

But, praise God, today I have been set free and healed of not only those memories but of the heart murmur as well! Today I can play baseball, basketball, and football and enjoy every minute of it. It is all because Jesus Christ became a curse for me. I am reaping the benefits of my relationship and covenant with Him.

DON'T ALLOW THE ENEMY'S LIES

It is true that Christians get sick and depressed. Christians some-times struggle with temper tantrums in the same way that their par-ents and grandparents struggled with hot tempers. Even Christians may be susceptible to a curse that has been passed down through the family line, continuing unchecked for generations. The beautiful truth for us to know is that we can be set free from those curses in Jesus' name. We do not have to wallow helplessly in a life-control-ling habit, sin, or curse.

Because of our disobedience to the Lord before we came to know Jesus, we deserve to experience the curse on our lives. However, because of faith in Jesus and the grace of God, we can rise up and walk in the freedom that comes from knowing Jesus Christ.

The devil has lied to many of us. He is the father of all lies (see John 8:44). Probably the devil has lied to you. Maybe he told you that you can't help yourself because the problems that you deal with are the same kind of problems and tendencies that you see in your parents. The truth is this: you may not have been able to help your-self before you received Jesus into your life, but when you were born again, things changed. You have a new Father in Heaven. Your new daddy is not under the curse. Your new Father in Heaven does not have temper tantrums. Your new Father in Heaven has not been struggling with cancer or migraine headaches or heart problems or whatever else may have "grown" into your family tree. Your new Father in Heaven will set you free from every curse.

Many times people "prophesy" over us in negative ways. Parents tell their children, "You're just like your dad; you have his bad tem-per"; or, "You'll never amount to anything." We can break these neg-ative "prophesies" in the name of Jesus Christ. They are a part of the curse. God loves you. He cares about you. That is why He went to the cross, so that all of our insecurities and fears and all those curses from past generations can be broken.

God wants to give you and me good gifts. James 1:17 tells us,

Every good and perfect gift is from above, coming down from the Father of the heavenly lights, who does not change like shifting shadows.

WE MUST STAKE OUR CLAIM

We know that Jesus came to set us free from every curse that the enemy wants to place in our lives. Romans 5:15,19 tells us that Adam brought sin and death, but that Christ brought grace and life;

For if the many died by the trespass of the one man [Adam], how much more did God's grace and the gift that came by the grace of the one man, Jesus Christ, overflow to the many! For just as through the disobedience of the one man [Adam] the many were made sinners, so also through the obedience of the one man [Jesus] the many will be made righteous.

Christ reclaimed what satan tried to take from us. We need to take back the areas of our lives that our enemy, the devil, has stolen from us.

The children of Israel went into Canaan, the new land that God promised to them. This new land was legally their land. God had told them clearly, "I'll give it to you." However, they had to go in and receive it, step by step. They had to walk in and claim it. Joshua 1:3 says,

I will give you every place where you set your foot, as I promised Moses.

In other words, God told Joshua, "Joshua, the land is yours, but you have to go in and claim it. You must take it back from your enemies." If the devil has stolen your peace, your joy, your health, or your hope, today is your day to claim it back from the enemy!

The children of Israel went to the city of Jericho, marched around it seven times, and shouted, and the walls came down. Even though it was theirs for the taking, they had to physically go in and claim it. You may say, "Well, I'm a Christian. Doesn't this all happen automatically?" Legally, yes, it's yours. But practically, in order to experience it, you need to go in and claim back from the devil the specific areas that he has stolen from you.

APPLY GOD'S WORD TO OUR LIVES

Christians have been delivered from the power of darkness and are now in Christ's Kingdom (see Col. 1:13). It is faith that unlocks the door. It is faith that makes the difference in our lives. Joshua was a man of faith. That's why he marched around the city of Jericho for seven days (see Josh. 6:14-15). As a man of faith, he obeyed God's Word and claimed the inheritance that the Lord had promised him. When we believe what God says in His Word, we will find ourselves being freed from depression, inferiority, insecurities, fears of mental illness, sickness, and disease. It is faith that unlocks the door. Romans 5:17 tells us clearly,

> *For if, by the trespass of the one man, death reigned through that one man, how much more will those who receive God's abundant provision of grace and of the gift of righteousness reign in life through the one man, Jesus Christ.*

God has called us to reign in life, to live a victorious life in Christ. If I give you a gift certificate for one thousand dollars, that gift certificate is worthless until you cash it in. The same is true of the Word of God. In order to walk victoriously in our spiritual lives, we have to seek, learn, and grow in the knowledge of God through His Word. We cannot grow without God's Word, and we cannot change without it. God's Word motivates us to obey and fellowship with Him. We need to take the Word of God and begin to apply it to every area of our lives so that we can experience the wholeness that God has promised. By doing so, we reclaim what the devil has tried to steal from us. God's Word is an indispensable weapon in Christian warfare against the devil.

Take the...sword of the Spirit, which is the word of God (Ephesians 6:17).

In Ephesians 6, we see that there are other items of Christian armor—the belt, the breastplate, the shoes, the shield, and the helmet—all intended for defense. The Word of God is the only weapon of attack. We must know God's Word and apply it to our lives so that we can attack the powers of darkness in our lives and put them to flight.

This may or may not happen overnight. God is a God of miracles, and He may move supernaturally and quickly to alter or heal a problem in our lives. But many times, He changes us through a more gradual process of growth and change. It takes more faith and character to persevere through problems, and God wants us to use His Word to overcome in this way.

To overcome life-dominating patterns in our lives or any other trial or temptation that confronts us, we need to be honest with God and confess our weakness and dependency on Him. As we confess the truth of God's Word, faith is built in our hearts (see Rom. 10:17). And as faith is built, we begin to experience the Lord's wholeness.

GUARD OUR TONGUES

We must be careful how we speak. Matthew 12:34 says, *"For out of the abundance of the heart the mouth speaks"* (NKJV). In other words, we believe with the heart, and what we speak is often what we really believe. The Bible also says that we will be judged by our words:

> *But I tell you that men will have to give account on the day of judgment for every careless word they have spoken. For by your words you will be acquitted, and by your words you will be condemned* (Matthew 12:36-37).

Life and death are in the power of the tongue (see Prov. 18:21). By our speech, we can pronounce either a blessing or a curse. If we continually say, "I think I'm going to get sick," we can begin to pronounce a curse of sickness on our lives. Instead we need to say, "I feel like I'm getting sick, but I know that God desires for me to be a whole person, and I can receive His healing." By speaking words of faith, we pronounce a blessing on our lives. When I wake up in the morning, I have learned to speak life to myself by confessing the Word of God. "I can do all things through Christ who strengthens me. Overwhelming victory is mine through Jesus Christ who loved me enough to die for me. Greater is He who is in me, than he that is in the world." And I experience the Lord's blessing throughout my day.

Sometimes people say, "My mother had a miscarriage; maybe I'll have a miscarriage too." By believing these words, we can begin to open the door for the devil to lay what we speak on our lives. The enemy will attempt to use these words to place fear in our lives, and the things that we fear can come upon us. Job 3:25 tells us, *"For the thing I greatly feared has come upon me, and what I dreaded has happened to me"* (NKJV). Fear is destroyed as we speak the Word of God to ourselves and to others around us. God tells us in Second Timothy 1:7, *"For God has not given us a spirit of fear, but of power and of love and of a sound mind"* (NKJV).

You may ask, "Why does it matter what we say, as long as our hearts are right?" Imagine walking into a bank with a toy water pistol and saying, "I'll take ten thousand dollars, please." The teller, seeing the gun, activates the alarm. The police rush in and arrest you. "I'm only kidding," you say. "It's only a water pistol. I was just joking. I didn't really mean it." Maybe you did not mean it, but you will end up in jail for the words you said and the action you took! The same principle applies to spiritual things. The devil is a legalist. He will use our words against us. We need to be careful how we speak. We need to speak the things that God says in His Word. We need to speak life-giving words that release hope in people's lives.

I have found that when I speak words of encouragement to people, it is often life-changing for them. The devil is lying to them all day long, and they are feeling discouraged and confused. A few words of encouragement will cause the cloud of encouragement and confusion to lift. Just today I was thanked by a pastor who had been struggling, and I was able to speak life and blessing to him.

RELEASE OUR INHERITANCE

Our God promises us wholeness, health, and victory in every area of our lives.

If you belong to Christ, then you are Abraham's seed, and heirs according to the promise (Galatians 3:29).

The Spirit Himself testifies with our spirit that we are God's children (Romans 8:16).

We are God's children through faith in Jesus Christ. God speaks to us by the Holy Spirit and tells us that we are heirs of His promises. He is the God who said that He would bless Abraham, and by faith you and I are also the children of Abraham. You may ask, "If I am really an heir of God, then why do I still deal with fear or confusion or depression?" We must remember, the New Testament is the new covenant or will that our Father in Heaven has left for us. If your uncle dies, and wills you his inheritance, you must sign the proper documents to release the inheritance before you can receive it. Spiritually, we must receive our inheritance from God in order to be set free.

We are free from the curse when we realize what the Word of God—the Lord's will and our inheritance—says and we act on it. For example, if you are feeling weak today, claim the strength that the Lord promises in His Word. The Bible says, "*I can do everything through Him who gives me strength*" (Phil. 4:13). Confess this promise and receive His strength today.

I was driving down the road in my car one day when a spirit of fear came on me like a cloud. I was paralyzed with fear. Immediately I was aware of what was happening. The enemy was trying to cause me to live by my feelings of fear rather than doing the things that I knew God was calling me to do. I said boldly, "In Jesus' name, I renounce this spirit of fear and command it to leave." And guess what? It left! When we resist the devil, he has to flee! (see James 4:7).

A few years ago, I was in Europe, alone in a guest bedroom in a friend's house, and experienced a similar spirit of fear. Again, this spirit of fear had to leave when I confronted it with the name of Jesus. Jesus Christ became a curse for us. We do not have to put up

DISCOVERING *the* BASIC TRUTHS *of* CHRISTIANITY

with a spirit of fear or any other affliction that the devil will try to bring against us. Jesus Christ has come to set us free.

RECLAIMING WHAT THE ENEMY STOLE
REFLECTION QUESTIONS

1. What does our covenant with Jesus Christ depend upon?

2. Has the devil lied to you about an area of your life in which you do not seem to have victory? What can you do about it?

3. How can the words that you say condemn you? Give examples from your life.

4. When we realize what our inheritance is, how do we release it? Speak Philippians 4:13 aloud.

Chapter 19

RECEIVING FREEDOM
IN JESUS' NAME

FREE SPIRITUALLY

In these next two chapters, we will look at seven areas of freedom that we can experience as believers in Jesus Christ. First of all, let's take a look at *spiritual freedom*. First John 1:9 says,

If we confess our sins, He is faithful and just and will forgive us our sins and purify us from all unrighteousness.

After we have given our lives to Jesus, the devil may try to paralyze us spiritually by telling us that we are not really saved. He is a liar! The Bible tells us in Romans 8:1-2, "*Therefore, there is now no condemnation for those who are in Christ Jesus, because through Christ Jesus the law of the Spirit of life set me free from the law of sin and death.*" There is no condemnation to those who are in Christ. And remember, there is a big difference between God's conviction and the enemy's condemnation. God's conviction always brings hope. But the devil's condemnation brings hopelessness.

The Bible tells us, "*For God is not a God of disorder but of peace...*" (1 Cor. 14:33). If your heart is turned toward the Lord and you are still experiencing spiritual doubts and confusion in your life, it is not from God. The devil is the author of confusion and condemnation. Jesus paid the price for this curse to be broken. I dealt with times of intense guilt after I gave my life to Jesus. One day, I got tired of it. I opened my Bible to First John 1:9, and declared to the devil, "I'm believing the Word of God, instead of what I feel in my emotions." Do you know what happened? I was set free. I later realized that the enemy had placed a curse over me. That curse of false guilt was trying to push me into depression, confusion, and frustration, but it was broken that night in Jesus' name.

I am reminded of the story of a farmer who was battling with false guilt and confusion in his life. He wasn't sure that he was saved. Finally, he went to the back of his barn, took a big stake, and hammered it into the ground. He confessed, "Jesus, You are the Lord of my life." He believed in his heart that Jesus was alive from the dead (see Rom. 10:9). Then He made a bold statement. "It happened right here at this stake. I gave my life completely to God. The next time the devil lies to me, I'm going right back here to this stake as proof. From this moment on, I will know that I know that I am saved!" How could he know? Because he knew that the curse of false guilt and confusion was broken because of Jesus Christ. He had made a decision to believe the truth, the Word of God. His life was different from that day on.

FREE FROM SICKNESS AND DISEASE

A second area of freedom has to do with freedom from sickness and disease. Physical healing is sometimes controversial in the Body of Christ. Let's see what the Bible has to say. Matthew 8:16-17 tells us,

When evening came, many who were demon-possessed were brought to Him, and He drove out the spirits with a word and healed all the sick. This was to fulfill what was spoken

through the prophet Isaiah: "He took up our infirmities and carried our diseases."

According to the New Testament, it is God's will that you and I are healed and healthy. When Jesus Christ went to the cross two thousand years ago, He provided forgiveness for sin, eternal, resurrection life for death, and *healing for sickness!* Freedom from the curse also includes the area of physical healing.

Jesus healed people who came to Him for healing. Matthew chapter 8 tells us that, when the people came to Him, He healed them. He was fulfilling the prophecy in the Old Testament from the book of Isaiah 53:4-5 that says, *"Surely He took up our infirmities...and by His wounds we are healed."* First Peter 2:24 says it similarly: *"He Himself bore our sins in His body on the tree, so that we might die to sins and live for righteousness; by His wounds you have been healed."*

While Jesus was teaching in a synagogue one Sabbath, He called a woman forward who was crippled by a spirit of infirmity. We should note here that, although Jesus healed many diseases, not all of them were attributed to demonic causes. However, in this case, it was. Jesus laid His hands on her, and immediately she was made straight and glorified God (see Luke 13:13). The ruler of the synagogue was indignant. He was not accustomed to this kind of thing happening in his religious meetings. Sometimes religious people have problems believing that we can be free from the curse of sickness and disease. Nevertheless, it could not be denied; Jesus Christ set the woman free. The same can happen today. The Bible tells us that Jesus Christ is the same yesterday, today, and forever (see Heb. 13:8).

Every sickness, every type of cancer, every case of heart failure, every migraine headache has been hung on the cross through Jesus Christ. We need to take God's Word seriously and place our faith in the Word of God instead of in the symptoms that we see in our bodies. We must seek the presence of Jesus in our lives and saturate our lives with God's Word. We should expect a miracle (see Matt. 7:8; 19:26).

I mentioned earlier in this book that I had a heart murmur as a young man. But a short time after coming to know Jesus Christ as Lord, my doctor found that I had been made completely whole. By the grace of God, I am completely free from any heart murmur today. Jesus Christ is our healer because He is the same yesterday, today, and forever.

HINDRANCES TO HEALING

Sometimes people say, "I know Jesus heals spiritually, but I'm not sure that He heals physically." The truth is that God wants to bless us with both.

Sometime back, a friend who owns a restaurant decided to treat our family to a meal. He told us that we could have anything we wanted on the menu, absolutely free. I had a choice to make. I did not deserve this free meal, yet I was told that I could not pay for it. As I looked at all of the sumptuous food, I could think, "I don't want to ask for too much. I don't want to take advantage of my friend." My friend would have been disappointed if I had responded that way, and it would have been pride keeping me from receiving a blessing. I believe the Lord responds to us the same way. God's only Son, Jesus Christ, went to the cross so that you and I could take advantage of the precious gift of wholeness that He has given to us. The entire bill has been paid!

Jesus Christ came to set you and me free from every curse, including the curse of sickness, disease, and all types of physical infirmities in our bodies. I have a friend who was miraculously healed of rheumatic fever. His parents decided to trust the Word of God to see their son healed, and although he was very sick, they chose to believe the Word of God instead of the symptoms that they saw. And he was healed! Jesus Christ came to set my friend free from the curse. The Bible says,

> *Praise the Lord, O my soul, and forget not all His benefits— who forgives all your sins and heals all your diseases* (Psalms 103:2-3).

God wants to heal all of our diseases, but sometimes there are hindrances to receiving divine healing, such as unconfessed sin (see James 5:16), demonic oppression or bondage (see Luke 13:11-13), fear or acute anxiety (see Prov. 3:5-8; Phil. 4:6-7), past disappoint- ments that undermine present faith (see Mark 5:26; John 5:5-7), unbiblical teaching (see Mark 3:1-5; 7:13), failure of the leaders to pray the prayer of faith (see Mark 11:22-24; James 5:14-16), failure of the Church to seek and obtain the gifts of miracles and healing as God intended (see Acts 4:29-30; 6:8; 8:5-6; 1 Cor. 12:9-10,29-31; Heb. 2:3-4), unbelief (see Mark 6:3-6; 9:19,23-24), or self-centered behavior (see 1 Cor. 11:29-30). At other times, the reason for the persistence of physical affliction in godly people is not readily appar- ent (see Gal. 4:13; 1 Tim. 5:23; 2 Tim. 4:20). In still other instances, God chooses to take His beloved saints to Heaven during an illness (see 2 Kings 13:14).[1]

If our prayers are not answered for healing, we cannot give up. We should rejoice if healing comes immediately and rejoice if it does not come at all (see Phil. 4:4). God promises never to forsake us or forget us. Sometimes God's purposes for us are for our greater good that we cannot understand.

If we believe that the Lord wants us to go to a doctor, then, by all means, we should go to a doctor. But let's go to our Great Physician first! The power of medical science is limited, but the power of God and His Word is unlimited! In the end, it is always Jesus, our Great Physician, who ultimately heals, anyway.

We are learning to live out the promises of God's Word in our Christian lives. We are learning to apply the promises of the Lord's inheritance to our lives. So we must chose to live by what God says in His Word, even though we may not see the expected results. Sometimes God tests our hearts to see if we really fear Him. He tested Abraham when He asked him to sacrifice Isaac (see Gen. 22:1-18). Job was tested, too, but in the end he prospered (see Job 42:10). God wants to set us free, but He also wants to know that we love Him more than we love any covenant blessing.

God is getting His Church to a place where we will walk together in wholeness and victory as we continue to grow in applying the Word of God to our lives. There are times when we need to do something specific, like calling for the elders of our church to pray for us and anoint us with oil:

Is any one of you sick? He should call the elders of the church to pray over him and anoint him with oil in the name of the Lord. And the prayer offered in faith will make the sick person well; the Lord will raise him up... (James 5:14-15).

The Bible tells us that, if we obey this scriptural mandate, the Lord will "raise us up"—heal us and make us completely whole by their prayer of faith.

FREE FROM PAINFUL MEMORIES

Many Christians long for a deeper and closer relationship with the Lord. But they continue to struggle with the same fears and hurtful memories from their past, unable to break free. Crippled emotionally, they need to be set free from the curse of painful memories and hurts in their lives. It is not God's will for people's hearts to be broken. He wants to heal us emotionally, according to Luke 4:18-19:

> *The Spirit of the Lord is on me, because He has anointed me to preach good news to the poor. He has sent me to proclaim freedom for the prisoners and recovery of sight for the blind,* **to release the oppressed,** *to proclaim the year of the Lord's favor.*

A young man and his fiancée came to me for premarital counseling. The young man had experienced many hurts in his life. For one, his father had constantly blamed him for the problems in his marriage because the son was conceived out of wedlock. The young man was hurting and needed healing. I asked him if he was willing to forgive his dad. He was willing. We laid hands on him and prayed for him to be healed of the painful memories that he received while growing up.

The young man had a wonderful wedding a few months later. His father was at his wedding, and there was no longer a wall between them. God had healed him. The pain was gone. God supernaturally healed him because Jesus Christ took that pain on the cross two thousand years ago. Jesus Christ became a curse for that young man.

Sometimes the term, "inner healing" is used to explain emotional healing. To receive inner healing means to be healed of lie-filled memories or to have our broken hearts healed. Sometimes our present emotional pain comes from the misinterpretations (lies) embedded in our memories and not from the memories themselves. For example, an incest victim feels shame not because she was molested but because she may believe it was her fault (a lie). When that lie is exposed, she can receive freedom!

Inner healing, or the healing of memories, is a very valid ministry in the Body of Christ today. If we believe that someone has hurt us and we continue to remember those hurts and the memories of what has happened, we need to be healed emotionally. We can be made whole! Jesus wants to heal us and set us free in His name.

The healing of memories does not mean that we no longer remember what has happened. We may remember what happened, but the pain has been healed through Jesus revealing the truth to us. We can look back and now give praise to God for His healing in our lives and His grace and strength to go on.

FORGIVE, FORGIVE, FORGIVE

We find an important scriptural key to being healed and set free in Matthew 6:14-15:

For if you forgive men when they sin against you, your heavenly Father will also forgive you. But if you do not forgive men their sins, your Father will not forgive your sins.

This is important! *We must forgive those who have hurt us in order for God to heal us.* In Matthew 18, Jesus tells a parable about a servant who owed his king one million dollars. When he begged the king for extra time to pay the debt, the king had pity on him and canceled the whole debt. The servant then went out and found one of his fellow servants who owed him two thousand dollars. He grabbed him by the shirt and demanded immediate payment. The fellow servant pleaded for more time, but the servant refused and had him thrown into prison. The king discovered what had happened and called the servant in. "I forgave you a million dollars, and you couldn't forgive someone a few thousand dollars? I showed you mercy, but you could not show mercy to another?" Then the Scripture makes an interesting statement:

> *In anger his master turned him over to the jailers to be tortured, until he should pay back all he owed. This is how my heavenly Father will treat each of you unless you forgive your brother from your heart* (Matthew 18:34-35).

The king had the man thrown into prison for not showing forgiveness to another. Jesus says that if we don't forgive someone who has hurt us or "ripped us off," God will deliver us to the *torturers* or *demons of hell.* Even Christians at times can be tormented with confusion, frustration, depression, etc. that is brought on by the demons of hell if they choose not to forgive. Unforgiveness leaves the door wide open for the devil.

I just returned from the nation of Rwanda where, in 1994, nearly one million persons were killed during the genocide. The pain was so great in families who lost their loved ones. But they realized that, in order to find healing and freedom, they had to forgive those who had murdered their family members. Today, these believers in Christ have found great freedom. In fact, some of the Christians are now going into the prisons and ministering Christ to those who had murdered their families. Forgiveness set them free.

Forgiving those who have hurt us is the first step to being set free. We may not feel like it, but because God forgave us, we need to forgive others in Jesus' name. God will bring emotional healing into our lives as we obey His Word and forgive in faith from our hearts.

FORGIVE SOME MORE

In addition to forgiving the person who has hurt us, we must also ask God to forgive the person. Asking God to forgive them is a vital second step of forgiveness that we need to take so that we can be set free. Stephen, when he was being stoned, said, "Father, forgive them" (see Acts 7:60). Jesus, on the cross, said, "Father, forgive them, they don't know what they do" (see Luke 23:34).

A third step is to ask God to forgive us for any wrong attitudes or attempts to hide our sin. Proverbs 28:13 says, "*He who conceals his sins does not prosper, but whoever confesses and renounces them finds mercy.*" The word *prosper* means "to break out" of bondage.[2] If we hide our sin and are not honest about it, we cannot break out of the bondage in our lives. If we don't ask God to heal us for wrong attitudes, then we cannot prosper in this area of our lives.

A fourth step is to confess our faults to someone and have him or her pray for us so that God will heal us. The Scripture says in James 5:16,

> *Therefore confess your sins to each other and pray for each other so that you may be healed. The prayer of a righteous man is powerful and effective.*

Ask someone to lay hands on you and pray for emotional healing. This is why it is so important to be connected to the rest of the Body of Christ through a local church. As you meet together with other believers, ask the Lord to show you someone whom you can trust to pray for you. The Lord wants to heal you and set you free from the curse in Jesus' name.

Corrie Ten Boom, who experienced life in a Nazi concentration camp and whose life story inspired the book and movie, *The Hiding Place*, had many opportunities to choose forgiveness. Listen to this account from a sermon by Dr. Ray Pritchard:

In one of her writings, Corrie Ten Boom, tells of some Christian friends who wronged her in a public and malicious way. For many days, she was bitter and angry until she forgave them. But in the night, she would wake up thinking about what they had done and get angry all over again. It seemed the memory would not go away. Help came in the form of a Lutheran pastor to whom she confessed her frustration after two sleepless weeks. He told her, "Corrie, up in the church tower is a bell that is rung by pulling on a rope. When the sexton pulls the rope, the bell peals out ding-dong, ding-dong. What happens if he doesn't pull the rope again? Slowly the sound fades away. Forgiveness is like that. When we forgive someone, we take our hand off the rope. But if we've been tugging at our grievances for a long time, we mustn't be surprised if the old angry thoughts keep coming for awhile. They're just the ding-dongs of the old bell slowing down."[3]

When you ask the Lord to heal you, the devil may try to bring some of those old emotions of hurt and pain back to you again and again. That is the time for you to say emphatically, "In Jesus' name, I know that He took my pain on the cross." As you declare the truth, the emotions of hurt feelings will dissipate as you focus on Jesus your healer instead of on the pain. In the same way that the sound from the big church bell rings loudly at first and then less and less, the memories of hurt will become less and less as you declare the truth that Jesus has healed you. In a very short time, you will get to the place where the devil cannot even tempt you anymore in this area. You will be completely and totally healed.

FREE TO HAVE A SOUND MIND

We live in a day of extreme stress. Many of us face mental anguish. Jesus came to set us free from this curse on our minds that has its root based in unwholesome fear. The Scriptures tell us in Second Timothy 1:7,

> *For God has not given us a spirit of fear, but of power and of love and of a sound mind* (NKJV).

God's purpose for your life is for you to have a sound mind. Perhaps your ancestors had some type of mental problems. God says that you can be free from that curse in Jesus' name. As I was growing up, I can vividly remember various members of my extended family who had a history of mental illness. I feared that I would spend periods of my life mentally ill in a mental hospital like some of my family members. One day I came to the realization that I didn't have to fear mental illness because Jesus Christ became a curse for me. By the grace of God, I have been freed from that curse.

The Lord's will for each of us is to have peace of mind. Isaiah 26:3 says,

You will keep in perfect peace him whose mind is steadfast, because he trusts in You.

Since I have been set free from the curse in Jesus' name, the Lord has delivered me from the fear of mental illness. We serve a good God! We can trust Him. He has promised us perfect peace as we continue to focus on our heavenly Father, the author of all peace (see 1 Cor. 14:33).

You and I are in a brand-new family, the family of God, through faith in Jesus Christ. We have a brand-new household, the household of God. Our new Father in Heaven does not have any mental problems at all.

We need to break every curse that is over our lives in Jesus' name. By the grace of God, I have broken every curse over my life in the name of Jesus. I am a free man! Today is your day of freedom. Today is the day for any curse over your life to be completely broken in Jesus' name.

ENDNOTES

1. The list of "hindrances to receiving divine healing" was taken from the *Full Life Study Bible* (Grand Rapids, MI: Zondervan, 1992), 1421.

2. *The Old Testament Hebrew Lexicon*, s.v. "Tsalach" (prosper), www.studylight.org/lex/heb/view.cgi?number=06743 (accessed 26 Sept 2008).

3. Dr. Ray Pritchard, "Is Total Forgiveness Realistic?" sermon, (Keep Believing Ministries, June 2003), www.keepbelieving.com/sermon/ 2003-06-01-Is-Total-Forgiveness-Realistic/+ding+dong+theory+corrie+ ten+boom&hl=en&ct=clnk&cd=3&gl=us (accessed 15 Sept 2008).

RECEIVING FREEDOM IN JESUS' NAME
REFLECTION QUESTIONS

1. Put your name in place of the words our and we in First Peter 2:24. Do you believe that God wants you to be free of every sickness and disease?

2. As an heir of all of the promises in the Bible, why wouldn't you want to take all that you can have? What should you do if your prayers for healing are not answered (see Phil. 4:4)?

3. Do you have painful memories of past hurts? Why do you think you are unable to break free?

4. If you are fearful, stressed out, and worried all of the time, Second Timothy 1:7 gives the solution. What is it?

Chapter 20

YOU CAN BE COMPLETELY FREE

FINANCIAL FREEDOM

In the previous chapter, we learned that we are redeemed from the curse in every facet of our existence. The curse is still in the world, but it has no right to be on us as Christians. We are redeemed from the curse. The curse on our spiritual, physical, emotional, and mental lives is removed by the blood of Jesus.

A fifth area of freedom that we can experience is financial freedom. Second Corinthians 8:9 says, *"For you know the grace of our Lord Jesus Christ, that though He was rich, yet for your sakes He became poor, so that you through His poverty might become rich."* God wants to prosper us in every way, including financially, so that we can give financially in order for the good news of Jesus to be taken throughout the whole world. Some people think it is godly to be poor. What they don't understand is that poverty is a part of the curse. If poverty is godly, then we should never be giving money to the poor. We would be hindering them from living in this godly state!

If you are struggling financially right now, I have good news for you. You don't have to be poor. God wants to prosper you. God wants to bless you and give you hope. Some people think that money is the root of evil. That's not exactly what the Scripture says in First Timothy 6:10. It says that the *love* of money is a root of evil. If we love money more than God, it is idolatry, and it leads us away from God.

It is wise to remember that prosperity and material things can never make us happy. Only Jesus can give us fulfillment and the abundant life. At the same time, the Lord desires to bless us. God wants to prosper us so that we can give to our families, the Church, and the poor, and see His Kingdom built throughout the whole world.

A lady, who was experiencing deep financial problems in her home, came to her pastor for help. Both her husband and her son were out of work. The pastor told her, "You need to read Galatians 3:13." He opened his Bible and read it to her, "*Christ redeemed us from the curse of the law by becoming a curse for us, for it is written: 'Cursed is everyone who is hung on a tree.'*"

"Jesus Christ became a curse for you," he explained to her, "so that you can be financially free." She came day after day for advice and counsel but didn't really listen.

Then about a year after she had first sought the pastor's advice, she came into his office and met with him once again. She said, "Guess what happened? I am finally prosperous. I was reading the Bible one day, and I received a revelation from God." She said, "It's Galatians 3:13." (This was the same truth that the pastor had been telling her over and over again, but this time she herself received a revelation from God.) She said, "Here's what happened. I realized that God wanted to prosper me. This poverty was a curse over my life. So, I went and got a job at a restaurant. The joy of the Lord was in my life, and I knew that the financial curse had been broken.

Later I bought the restaurant." She is a prosperous woman today because the favor of God is on her. In fact, people come back just because of the godly atmosphere in her restaurant. The Scriptures tell us in Ephesians 4:28,

> *He who has been stealing must steal no longer, but must work, doing something useful with his own hands, that he may have something to share with those in need.*

Jesus wants to bless us so that we can give to others. As we work with an attitude of freedom and joy, we will experience the Lord's blessing. The curse has been broken. The Lord desires to prosper you as you obey Him.

SOCIAL FREEDOM

A sixth area of freedom from the curse is social freedom. God wants us to have good success in every realm and area of our life, including the way in which we relate to people socially. When I was growing up, I had a hard time looking people in the eye because I felt inferior. It was a curse that had to be broken. Today, by the grace of God, I love to meet people. The curse of being afraid to face people is gone in Jesus' name! According to the Bible, being afraid of people is a trap! But when we really trust the Lord, we can find safety in our relationships:

> *Fear of man will prove to be a snare, but whoever trusts in the Lord is kept safe* (Proverbs 29:25).

Jesus had great favor with the people of His day. Wherever Jesus went, *"the common people heard Him gladly"* (Mark 12:37 NKJV). I believe Jesus was really fun to be with. Children loved to be with Jesus (see Matt. 18:2-5).

God wants you and me to be able to relate to other people in a positive way. A curse that may be over you from generations past will hinder you from relating to people in a sociable and loving way. Jesus has liberated us from that horrible harvest of sin that can affect generations. That curse needs to be broken today in the name of Jesus. Jesus Christ became a curse for you!

This does not mean that we will escape persecution or that everyone will like us. Persecution may take many forms. In some countries today, Christians are tortured and imprisoned for their beliefs. I was recently in such a nation, meeting with Christian leaders, most of whom had been in prison for their faith. Other times, Christians may be deprived of a job for which they are eligible or held up to ridicule at work or school, all because of their religious persuasion. Second Timothy 3:12 tells us that we will all experience some kind of persecution if we truly live godly lives: *"In fact, everyone who wants to live a godly life in Christ Jesus will be persecuted."*

Jesus instructed us to rejoice when others say all kinds of evil against us falsely for His sake (see Matt. 5:11-12), and yet, the Bible tells us that people in the early Church had favor with all of the people and that people were coming to know Jesus Christ every day (see Acts 2:47). Are you finding God's favor on your life? The Lord's desire is for you to experience the favor of the Lord. Take a close look at Psalm 5:12:

> *For surely, O Lord, You bless the righteous; You surround them with Your favor as with a shield.*

God desires to surround you with His favor today. Declare your freedom from the curse through Jesus Christ. The price of redemption is paid. Receive it for yourself. Today is your day of freedom.

FREEDOM FROM DEMONIC ACTIVITY

A seventh area of freedom is freedom from demonic activity. The word "demon possessed" in New Testament Greek is the word *demonized* which means "to have a demon."[1] People throughout the New Testament often suffered from satan's oppression and influence because of an indwelling evil spirit. Jesus and the New Testament Christians were constantly casting demons out of people:

> *When evening came, many who were demon-possessed were brought to Him, and He drove out the spirits with a word and healed all the sick* (Matthew 8:16).

In our modern society, people often are too sophisticated to believe that individuals can have demons. Some people don't even believe in demons. The Bible tells us, however, that demons are evil spirits who are enemies of God and humans (see Matt. 12:43-45). In addition, they can live in the bodies of unbelievers to enslave them to immorality and evil (see Mark 5:15; Luke 4:41; 8:27-28; Acts 16:18), and they can cause physical illness (see Matt. 4:24; Luke 5:12-13), although not all illness is the result of evil spirits.

Whether people want to believe it or not, the truth is, many people today are tormented by demons. Those involved in magic or spiritism using Ouija boards, seances, tarot cards, or horoscopes are dealing with evil spirits and can be led into demonic bondage. Demonic activity in their lives may express itself in fits of anger, confusion, violence, immorality, or depression, to name a few.

People sometimes ask me if Christians can have demonic activity in their lives. Yes, they can, but it doesn't mean that they are demon possessed or under the complete control of a demon. However, demons may have influence in Christians' thoughts and emotions and actions when they fail to submit to the Holy Spirit's leading in their lives.

I was speaking to a Christian leader who told me that he had a demon of anger cast out of his life. He had gone through times of uncontrollable anger and didn't understand why. Finally one day, he confided in a pastor who took authority over the demon and cast it out in Jesus' name. He has not been the same since. Today he is one of the gentlest men I have ever met. Jesus Christ set him free.

Although satan constantly wars against God's people, trying to draw them away from their loyalty to Christ, Jesus promised believers authority over the power of satan and his demons. He became a curse for us so that we can be free from any type of demonic spirit influencing our lives. We do not have to fear the powers of darkness. Years ago, a man in a backslidden state came to me and said, "Larry, I want you to know that I have used a voodoo doll and have placed a curse on you." There was no fear in my heart when he said that. Do you know why? Because I knew that Jesus Christ became a curse for me. A curse could not be placed on me because I was protected by the blood of Jesus Christ:

> *They overcame him by the blood of the Lamb...* (Revelation 12:11).

As Christians, we live by faith in the Word of God. We are living under His grace and are protected with God's law of protection from the enemy through Christ! As Christians, we have power over satan because of what Jesus did on the cross. He shattered the power of satan's realm when He died and rose again. He disarmed satan.

The Bible says, *"For God has not given us a spirit of fear..."* (2 Tim. 1:7 NKJV). If we have a paralyzing fear of satan and his evil intentions, we are not just fearful; we have a spirit of fear. A spirit of fear can be a demonic spirit of deception. Satan is the author of fear and wants us to walk in fear. Demonic spirits of all kinds must be resisted and commanded to leave in Jesus' name. We can break the power they attempt to exert over us. If we are dealing with a violent temper, depression, a sudden compulsion to commit suicide, or other life-dominating problems, these very well may be demonic spirits that are controlling our lives. We cannot be oblivious to their deception. We must be alert to satan's schemes and temptations and desire to be set free.

RESIST THE DEVIL; HE WILL FLEE

To be set free from demonic bondage, we must resist the devil by prayer and proclaim God's Word as we call upon the mighty name of Jesus. A friend told me that he once sensed a strange, evil presence at a friend's house. Calling upon the name of Jesus Christ, a few Christian believers prayed and took authority over a curse that needed to be broken over that home. The evil presence left. James 4:7 says,

Submit yourselves, then, to God. Resist the devil, and he will flee from you.

Smith Wigglesworth was an evangelist in Great Britain years ago. He once told the story of a woman whose pet dog had followed her to the bus-stop and wouldn't go home until she finally "stamped her foot and said severely: 'Go home at once!' The dog immediately took off home, with its tail between its legs." Wigglesworth, who had been watching this interaction, said, "'That's how you have to treat the devil'…loudly enough for all those waiting at the bus-stop to hear."[2] Like the pet dog in Wigglesworth's story, unless we firmly resist the devil, he will continue to hang around with his "yelping" and aggravation. But if we boldly tell him to leave us alone, he will flee. The devil has no choice when we resist him in Jesus' name. He must flee.

As Christians, we can call upon Jesus to defeat satan and his demonic powers. Matthew 12:29-30 says that we can tie up the strong man (satan) and rob his house (set free those who are enslaved to satan):

> *Or again, how can anyone enter a strong man's house and carry off his possessions unless he first ties up the strong man? Then he can rob his house* (Matthew 12:29-30).

We can drive demons out in the name of Jesus by "tying up" the demonic spirit who is influencing our lives or someone else's life. Only then can we be free. As believers, we can provide deliverance for those who have been held captive by satan's power:

> *And these signs will accompany those who believe: In my name they will drive out demons; they will speak in new tongues* (Mark 16:17).

Casting out demons is a ministry that the Lord has given to those who believe in Him. Christians are called to minister deliverance to those bound by satan. If you believe that the Lord is calling you to set people free from demonic spirits, I encourage you to follow the example of Jesus. Jesus sent His disciples out two by two to minister, and they came back excited! Why? "*...Even the demons submit to us in your name!' they said*" (Luke 10:17).

We should note that Jesus gives His disciples a word of caution, "*...do not rejoice that the spirits submit to you, but rejoice that your names are written in heaven*" (Luke 10:20). Jesus cautioned the disciples not to make the power over the demons the source of their joy but to rejoice because of their relationship with Him.

The fact remained—demons could not stand in the presence of the disciples who were commissioned by Jesus to cast them out. The Lord has also commissioned us to cast demons out of people and to be set free from demonic activity in our own lives in Jesus' powerful name.

RENOUNCE DEMONIC SPIRITS

Sometimes people get involved innocently with the demonic by dabbling in paranormal energies in order to gain knowledge of the future or to uncover secrets—reading tarot cards, playing demonic games like the Ouija board, water witching to detect hidden water sources, attending seances to contact the dead, using of drugs to produce "spiritual experiences"—all of these kinds of practices are associated with the occult. Attempting to communicate with the supernatural through these kinds of methods is actually communication with demons (see 1 Sam. 28:8-14; 2 Kings 21:6; Isa. 8:19).

Getting involved in these kinds of occult practices is dangerous and can lead to demonic bondage. The Bible gives these warnings:

...Do not practice divination or sorcery (Leviticus 19:26).

Do not turn to mediums or seek out spiritists, for you will be defiled by them. I am the Lord your God (Leviticus 19:31).

As a young boy, I participated in a type of *divination* by trying to "smell for water" on our family farm. We believed that, by holding a rod, we could locate underground streams of water, thus knowing where to drill a well. Although I was completely unaware of it at the time, I was dabbling in the occult. Trying to uncover the unknown forces of nature by using superstitious practices like this is really opening ourselves to demonic spirits. After I received Jesus Christ as Lord, I claimed my freedom from the curse that the enemy tried to place over my life through my involvement in this occult practice. Years ago, I also played with an Ouija board, a game that attempts to uncover secret things by submitting to unknown spiritual forces. Again, I broke that curse over my life in the name of Jesus Christ.

There are two supernatural powers—the power of God through Jesus Christ and the power of the enemy. A curse can be placed over our lives if we are involved in any type of occult practices. I have ministered to people who had an intense desire to commit suicide or fell into depression because the devil held them in bondage due to their involvement in the occult. The good news is this! You can be set completely free. If you or your ancestors have been involved in any type of occult activity, you can be set free. When you renounce those demonic spirits in the name of Jesus, the demons can no longer have any control of your life.

A friend of ours had migraine headaches for more than eight years. In her case, this physical ailment was tied to her involvement in the occult. In desperation, she went to some Christians for help. They rebuked the devil in Jesus' name, and she was set free from the curse of constant headaches over her life.

Our lives are like an onion with many layers of skin. Maybe you have been set free from demonic spirits in your life. There may be little layers that God has already peeled off. However, the Lord may take you through other areas of freedom in the future.

He loves us and takes us step by step. He knows what we can handle. As the Lord reveals other areas of bondage in our lives, we receive His freedom. Then another layer comes off. The Lord continues this process until we are completely clean and are the people He has called us to be. He is committed to seeing us set completely free. This process may take days, months, or even years.

FREE FROM FAMILY CURSES

Earlier in this book, we mentioned generational (family) curses that may be passed down through the generations. Unrepented sin can leave a spiritual weakness toward a particular sin in a family line. For example, a sexual sin may produce a curse. The curse then causes a generational weakness to that sin to be passed down in the family line. If the sin is not made right before God, it continues its pattern and strongly influences our lives.

Generational sins cause spiritual *strongholds* or mindsets that cause us to say, "Even God cannot change this circumstance in my life. It's hopeless." We begin to accept this lie and fall into sin that produces a viselike grip in our lives. There are multitudes of strongholds that can be passed through family lines: addictions like alcohol, food, compulsive spending; mental problems like depression, rage, worry; sexual problems like homosexuality, fornication, pornography; and heart issues that include bitterness, greed, rebellion, legalism, and gossip.

First, it is important to identify the strongholds that afflict our family lines before we can break these strongly fortified holds on our lives.

The weapons we fight with are not the weapons of the world. On the contrary, they have divine power to demolish strongholds. We demolish arguments and every pretension that sets itself up against the knowledge of God, and we take captive every thought to make it obedient to Christ (2 Corinthians 10:4-5).

Next, we should repent of our own sin. Even though we have inherited a spiritual weakness to a particular sin in our family, it is no excuse for the sin that we have committed. Then, we forgive our ancestors for bringing the sin into the family line: "*If you forgive anyone his sins, they are forgiven; if you do not forgive them, they are not forgiven"* (John 20:23). We cannot harbor unforgiveness in our hearts. Finally, we need to repent of (or renounce) the sin. By doing so, we break the power of that sin in our generation. We remove satan's legal right to continue plaguing us and our children in that particular area.

OUR SPIRITUAL WEAPONS

As Christians, we are engaged in a spiritual conflict with evil. Although we have been guaranteed victory through Christ's death on the cross, we must wage spiritual warfare by the power of the Holy Spirit using our spiritual armor (see Eph. 6:10-18).

One time, the disciples could not cast out a demon in a young boy, and Jesus said, *"this kind can come out only by prayer ["and fasting,"* in some translations]" (Mark 9:29).

Jesus implied that if His disciples had maintained a life of prayer, like He did, they could have successfully cast this demon out. When we recognize that we are in conflict against spiritual forces and powers of evil, we will live fervently before God and be equipped by faith to see others delivered from demonic spirits.

To overcome evil, God has given us weapons. The first weapon is the "name of Jesus Christ." The Scriptures tell us

That at the name of Jesus every knee should bow, in heaven and on earth and under the earth, and every tongue confess that Jesus Christ is Lord, to the glory of God the Father (Philippians 2:10-11).

Some time ago, I was awakened in the night and sensed an evil presence in my room. I was away from home, and no one else was in the house where I was staying. I felt like I was frozen to my bed. I could only call out the name of "Jesus." The evil presence left, and I was able to go back to sleep. There is power in the name of Jesus.

The second weapon that the Lord has given to us against the enemy is the blood of Jesus Christ. I have actually witnessed demons in people who have shrieked in fear at the mention of the blood of Jesus. On one occasion, a man with demons held his hands over his ears and screamed when the blood of Jesus was mentioned. The blood of the Lamb has freed us from the power of the enemy. The Scriptures tell us in Revelation 12:11,

> *they overcame him by the blood of the Lamb and by the word of their testimony; they did not love their lives so much as to shrink from death* (Revelation 12:11).

The third weapon that the Lord has given to us against the curse of the enemy is the word of our testimony. Our testimony is simply confessing what the Lord has done in our lives and what God is saying about us. We know what God says about us by believing His Word. The truth of God's Word sets us free.

In closing, I am going to ask you to pray the following prayer aloud. We will confess the Word of God and our testimony and find freedom from the curse in Jesus' name.

> *In the name of Jesus Christ, I renounce any involvement that I or my family has ever had with the occult back to the third and fourth generation in Jesus' name. I declare that I am a child of the living God through faith in Jesus Christ. Jesus Christ is the Lord and King of my life. His blood has cleansed me from every sin and from every curse that the enemy would have tried to place against my life. The Bible says, "whom the Son sets free is free indeed" (see John 8:36). I am free today*

in the mighty name of Jesus. I declare my freedom from spiritual bondage and false guilt in Jesus' name. I declare freedom today from any type of physical illness or disease in the name of Jesus. I declare that I am emotionally whole in the name of Jesus Christ. I forgive anyone who has ever hurt me in Jesus' name. I declare that I am free mentally in the name of Jesus. I declare that I am free financially and that I shall prosper in Jesus' name. I declare in the name of Jesus that I am free socially and that the favor of God is on my life. I declare that I am free from every demonic stronghold and strategy of the enemy in the name of Jesus. The strong man has been bound in Jesus' name, and Jesus Christ has set me free. I declare that the blood of Jesus Christ has set me free! I claim my inheritance according to the Word of God that Jesus Christ has become a curse for me. I thank you for it in Jesus' name. Amen."

If you feel that you need to have another person pray with you and take authority over any demonic spirit or influence in your life, do it! The Lord will be faithful to lead you to the right person. This Spirit-filled believer in Jesus Christ, who has an intimate relationship with Jesus, can pray for you, and the Lord will set you free.

ENDNOTES

1. *The New Testament Greek Lexicon*, s.v. "Daimonizomai" (demonized), www.studylight.org/lex/grk/view.cgi?number=1139 (accessed 26 Sept 2008).

2. Andrew Strom and Larry Magnello, "Great Healing Revivalists—How God's Power Came" *Revival School*, 1996, 2004, www.revivalschool.com/books/GREAT%20HEALING%20REVIVALISTS.htm (accessed 26 Sept 2008).

You Can Be Completely Free
Reflection Questions

1. Is it godly to be poor? Who does God want to use to spread the Gospel and meet the needs of millions in the world?

2. What does Psalm 5:12 say that God wants to surround us with?

3. What dangers must we be aware of when someone is involved in the supernatural apart from Christ? How do occult practices affect the lives of those involved?

4. Identify any generational sins in your family line. Write them down and walk through the steps of repentance and forgiveness mentioned above.

PART VI

Living in the Grace of God

Chapter 21

WHAT IS GRACE?

GRACE AFFECTS EVERYTHING

The Denver Zoo acquired a polar bear:

> They built a temporary cage for the bear until its naturalistic environment could be constructed. The cage was just wide enough that the bear could walk several steps in one direction, whirl around, and take several steps in the opposite direction, back and forth. When the bear's environment was finally constructed and the cage removed, the bear continued to walk back and forth within the old punctuation.[1]

The bear was only supposed to stay in his cage for several weeks, but while the zoo built his new environment, set backs occurred. So instead of a few weeks, the bear spent several months in his tiny cage, being able to walk only three steps from end to end. When the bear was finally set free in his new environment, out of habit, he continued to walk three steps to the right, whirl around and walk three steps to the left. Even when he was free of his physical borders, he "framed" himself in imaginary borders.

Some Christians find themselves in a similar dilemma. Having become so accustomed to certain thought patterns of defeat and failure in some areas of their lives, they convince themselves that things will never change and that they are locked in an invisible, mental prison.

Precious, born again, Spirit-filled Christians who love Jesus with all of their hearts are susceptible to this kind of mental trap. Some, upon facing incredible obstacles in their lives, become weary and settle for far less than the Lord intended for them.

Years ago, I received a revelation from the Lord about the grace of God that has literally revolutionized my life. Although I was in love with Jesus and filled with the Holy Spirit, I was still living in a mental prison. It seemed like some things would never change. Then one day someone vividly described the "grace of God" to me in a way that literally changed my life. God's grace offered in the Scriptures goes far beyond what is offered by other world religions. Many religions say that man gets what he deserves. Others add that man does not get all that he deserves (mercy). Grace goes way beyond that idea, however. Grace is God's unimaginable and total kindness. We receive it freely and do not deserve it, and our hearts cannot but change because of it. We cannot fully describe it, but we can experience it. Grace affects everything that we do in life. When I finally began to understand the grace of God, it changed the way that I thought, acted, and responded to difficulties that arose in my life.

Grace is mentioned more than 156 times in the New Testament.[2] Since grace is mentioned so often, we need to understand what the grace of God is really about and how it affects our lives. Paul, the apostle, while writing to the Church, often began his letters speaking about grace. He would also close his letters with, "The grace of the Lord Jesus be with you." He continually emphasized *grace* throughout the New Testament.

Grace and peace to you from God our Father and the Lord Jesus Christ. I always thank God for you because of His grace given you in Christ Jesus (1 Corinthians 1:3-4).

GOD'S FREE GIFT OF SALVATION

Grace is sometimes defined as the free, unmerited favor of God on the undeserving and ill-deserving. God loves us and does not want us to be separated from Him by sin. So our first glimpse of grace occurs when God offers salvation to us even though we do not deserve it or work to earn it. He gives a measure of grace as a gift to unbelievers so that they may be able to believe in the Lord Jesus. Ephesians 2:8-9 says,

For it is by grace you have been saved, through faith—and this not from yourselves, it is the gift of God—not by works, so that no one can boast.

We come to God initially because He is the One who has drawn us. Jesus says in John 6:44, "*No one can come to Me unless the Father who has sent Me draws him.*" I've met people who have said, "I found God." We do not find God; He finds us! He has been drawing us to Himself all along. The reason that we are Christians is simply because of God's grace and goodness in our lives. God has given us His grace because of His infinite goodness. God is good! And because He is good and He loves us so much, He gives us the free gift of grace—and draws us to Himself—and we are saved. We don't deserve to be saved, but God freely extends His grace to us. Romans 11:6 says,

And if by grace, then it is no longer by works; if it were, grace would no longer be grace.

It is grace that motivates God to offer us salvation. We cannot earn it; it is a gift. So we see that our salvation comes as a gift of God's grace, and it can be accessed by our response of faith.

Grace could be described as a coin with two distinct sides to it. We just described the one side of the coin that is characterized by the saving grace of God—"the free unmerited favor of God on the undeserving and ill-deserving." The other side of the grace coin is the grace that God gives to believers to give them the "desire and the power to do God's will." We will look at this aspect of grace a bit later in this book. Both aspects of grace encompass the whole of the Christian life from the beginning to the end. We are totally dependent on the grace of God.

MERCY VS. GRACE

There is a difference between God's grace and mercy. Sometimes we get these two terms confused. God's *mercy* is "God not giving us what we deserve" and God's *grace* is "God giving us those things that we do not deserve."

We deserve hell, sickness, disease, and troubles because our sin places us in darkness. Yet, even though we do not deserve it, God offers us forgiveness, peace, eternal life, hope, healing, and the Holy Spirit; the list goes on—all because of His wonderful grace!

A few years ago, I was traveling through a small town in the Midwest with my family. I was not aware that the speed limit was 25 miles per hour, and I was traveling 35 miles per hour. As I got to the other side of the town, I heard a shrill siren behind me. Sure enough, it was a policeman, signaling me to pull off to the side of the road. He then proceeded to write up a traffic ticket as he fulfilled his responsibility as a police officer. Now, if the policeman would have been exercising mercy, he would have said, "Look, I understand that you didn't realize that you were going 10 m.p.h. over the limit. I'll allow you to go free." If he would have been operating in a principle of grace, he would have said, "You are a really nice guy. In fact, I like you so much I'd like to give you a hundred dollars just for traveling on our streets." Unfortunately for me, he did not operate in mercy or grace, but he did allow me to receive *justice*—he gave me a ticket with a fine to pay!

I can remember, early in my Christian life, that I felt like God somehow owed me a nice family and a prosperous life, complete with a paycheck each week. After all, I thought, I had worked for it. I didn't realize how arrogant I was. If it wasn't for the grace of God, I would not have the physical strength or health to work in the first place. God didn't owe me anything. First He had shown mercy to me and saved me, then He showered His grace on me, giving me those things that I did not deserve—God's wonderful presence in my life through Jesus Christ.

Christ Jesus came into the world to save sinners—of whom I am the worst. But for that very reason I was shown mercy so that in me, the worst of sinners, Christ Jesus might display His unlimited patience as an example for those who would believe on Him and receive eternal life (1 Timothy 1:15-17).

NO LONGER UNDER THE LAW

God gave Moses moral laws to follow (the Ten Commandments) that were given to show men their sinful condition. The law showed the human race the difference between right and wrong. Through attempting to obey the law, mankind sought to earn the blessing of God by what they did.

Then Jesus came and changed all of that. Through Him we are offered grace—the free, undeserving favor of God that comes through faith in Jesus, who is the Truth. When a person trusts Christ for salvation, his righteousness no longer depends on keeping the law. Since the Christian is under grace, he cannot be under the law. The Bible says that grace and truth came through Jesus Christ:

> *For the law was given through Moses; grace and truth came through Jesus Christ* (John 1:17).

Those under the law are always conscious of the power of sin within themselves, frustrating them from living victoriously. Those observing the law must observe all its requirements at all times because, if they break even one point, they break the whole law (see James 2:10). We cannot become righteous from keeping the law; in fact, it is impossible to keep the law. We all stand self-condemned because we fall short of obeying the law. The only escape is to come out from under the law. That is why we are righteous only by faith in Christ. To escape the dominion of sin, a Christian comes out from under the law and comes under grace:

> *For sin shall not be your master, because you are not under law, but under grace* (Romans 6:14).

THE TEN COMMANDMENTS

Let's take a brief look at the Ten Commandments (see Deut. 5:6-21) to see how far every person falls short of keeping the law. The law helps us to see how important grace is to our lives.

1. **You shall have no other gods before Me.**

   We break this law every time we give something or some-one other than God complete first place in our affections. No man or woman has ever kept this commandment.

2. **You shall not make for yourself a graven image.**

   It is impossible for an image or picture of God to truly represent God and all of His glory. If we approach God with our lips, but not our hearts, we have a false image of Him and are far from Him (see Mark 7:6).

3. **You shall not take the name of the Lord your God in vain.**

   Most times, we think of using the Lord's name in a profane utterance as "taking His name in vain." But if we call Him *Lord* and disobey Him, we are taking His name in vain. If we are filled with fear and doubts, we deny His name.

4. **Remember the sabbath day, to keep it holy.**

   God's plan was to give men and women a day of rest so that they could worship undistracted. Christ takes our burdens and gives us a spiritual rest or "Sabbath-rest" (see Heb. 4:10), but often we fail to enter into that rest.

5. **Honor your father and your mother.**

   Parents represent God's authority to their children. Yet children are often disrespectful and ungrateful to their parents.

6. **You shall not kill.**

   Jesus said that to be angry with another without a cause and to be insulting are just as serious as murder (see Matt.

5:21-22). We can murder others by gossip, neglect, cruelty, or jealousy.

7. **You shall not commit adultery.**

This commandment not only includes sex outside of marriage, but also such sins as entertaining adulterous thoughts, looking at pornography, submitting to impure fantasies, selfish demands in marriage, flirting, etc. (See Matthew 5:27-28.)

8. **You shall not steal.**

Evading income tax is stealing. Working short hours for an employer is stealing. An employer who underpays his workers steals from them.

9. **You shall not bear false witness against your neighbor.**

This refers not only to what could happen in a court of law, but it also includes all kinds of idle talk, lies, exaggerations, gossip, or even making jokes at another's expense.

10. **You shall not covet.**

Covetousness happens in the heart and mind. When we are jealous of someone's house or lifestyle or spouse or car, we are enslaved to covetousness.

The Ten Commandments convince us of our sinfulness and inability to keep the righteous law of God. As important as the Ten Commandments are, we simply cannot keep these rules on our own. We need a Savior. Jesus came as the remedy for our sin. Sin does not have dominion over Christians because we are not under the law. We are under grace.

GRACE IS MORE POWERFUL THAN SIN

God's moral law, the Ten Commandments, is important because it shows mankind the true nature of sin. When we see the extent of our failure to obey God's laws, we see more clearly God's abounding grace in forgiving us! The Bible says, "*...but where sin increased, grace increased all the more*" (Rom. 5:20).

Grace is much more powerful than sin! Romans 5:21 goes on to say that sin used to rule over all men and bring them to death, but now God's kindness rules instead, giving us right standing with God and resulting in eternal life through Jesus Christ. Wherever you find sin and disobedience, you will find God's grace available.

The Holy Spirit works within believers to allow them to live lives of righteousness. This is a fulfillment of God's moral law. We cannot do it on our own, but only by God's grace. So grace and obedience to God's law are not in conflict. They both point to righteousness and holiness. We are able to live holy lives and to keep God's moral codes only by His grace.

Many years ago, I drove a little Volkswagen "bug." One day, the car stopped running. I decided that I had enough of a mechanical background to enable me to take the motor out and fix it. But I soon realized that I was getting nowhere fast. I certainly was trying, but I knew that I needed help. I towed it to a garage where a mechanic fixed it! Without the grace of God, we cannot fix ourselves. Did I deserve to have the Volkswagen fixed? No, but it ran again because of God's grace and because of the grace on the mechanic who fixed it. It is God's grace that saves us from sin and puts us back together.

If we make a mistake, we confess it to God and move ahead by the grace of God, knowing that it's His grace that gives us the strength to go on. Why does God forgive us? He forgives us because of His gift of grace. Why does God fill us with the Holy Spirit? We're filled because of the grace of God. Even if we have made a mess of our lives, we can find forgiveness and move on because of the grace of God.

CHEAP GRACE?

If God is willing to forgive sin, and since Christians are under grace and not the law, does this mean that we can continue to tolerate sin in our lives and yet remain secure from judgment? After all, God's grace pardons sin. We can sin because God will always forgive us, right? Wrong! This is the very issue that the early Church ran into. Paul challenges this train of thought that "cheapens" God's grace:

> *What shall we say, then? Shall we go on sinning so that grace may increase? By no means! We died to sin; how can we live in it any longer?* (Romans 6:1-2).

It is a distortion of God's grace to think that we can continue to live in sin and that God's grace will cover it. The Bible tells us in First John 3:4 that *"everyone who sins breaks the law, in fact, sin is lawlessness."* When we came to Christ, we made a separation from sin—we died to sin's power and control over our lives. As Christians, we are freed from sin's power so that we can walk in newness of life (see Rom. 6:4-5,10). We are no longer slaves to sin.

Yet, every believer must be careful to daily reaffirm his decision to resist sin and follow Christ (see Rom. 8:13; Heb. 3:7-11). Known sin in our lives grieves the Holy Spirit and quenches His power (see Eph. 4:30; 1 Thess. 5:19). If we keep returning to sin and cease to resist it, eventually our hearts will grow hard and unyielding. It is possible (because of the hardening that can take place in our hearts because of sin—see Heb. 3:8) to reach a place in the downward spiral of rebellion and disobedience when we no longer really believe in anything. We become sin's slave again with death as its result: *"For the wages of sin is death..."* (Rom. 6:23).

Although God's grace gives us power to resist sin, it is true that, while living our day-to-day lives, we will not always consistently resist sin. When we fail, our God of grace and mercy is willing to forgive us. When we mess up our lives and go back to God, God's grace is freely extended. However, we should be cautioned against thinking that we can sin because we are under grace. Remember, there may be a point of no return.

ENDNOTES

1. Bradford P. Keeney, *Aesthetics of Change*, (New York: Guilford Press, 2002), 48.

2. Paul R. McReynolds, *Word Study Greek-English New Testament* (Carol Stream, IL: Tyndale House Publishers, 1999).

WHAT IS GRACE?
REFLECTION QUESTIONS

1. Like the bear in the cage, are you held captive to any old habits or deceptions?

2. What are some things that God gave you because of His grace? What are some things that He did not give you because of His mercy?

3. The law came through Moses, but what came through Jesus Christ, according to John 1:17? How do we escape the law and come under grace?

4. What increases with sin, according to Romans 5:20? How have you experienced this in your life?

Chapter 22

RESPONDING
to GOD'S GRACE

TOTALLY DEPENDENT ON GOD'S GRACE

Paul, the apostle, went through years of theological training and had an impeccable background of pure Jewish descent. Yet he says that all of his advantages of birth, education, and personal achievement can be attributed to the grace of God:

But by the grace of God I am what I am, and His grace to me was not without effect. No, I worked harder than all of them—yet not I, but the grace of God that was with me (1 Corinthians 15:10).

If we think we are strong spiritually or a fantastic husband or a good student or a mature single, we must remember that our strength is not in ourselves, but in Jesus Christ. Like Paul, we are totally dependent on the grace of God. Everything that we have, everything that we will ever do, everything that we are, is simply by the grace of God.

When we understand how grace works in our lives, we will find ourselves living with a new freedom in our daily relationship with Jesus. Every good thing in our lives is a result of the grace of God. You and I really do not deserve anything. If you have good health today, it is because of the grace of God. Any gift or ability that you have can be credited to the grace of God. If you are an excellent parent, it is not because you are so talented with children, but it is the grace of God that enables you to be a good parent. If you are a fantastic basketball player, it's because of the grace of God. You may say, "But I practice." Who gave you the ability and health to practice? God did. Good students are recipients of the grace of God. If you are a financially secure businessman, the grace of God is the reason that you are successful. When we get this truth into our spirits and live out the grace of God, it totally revolutionizes us. It changes us from the inside out.

The devil cannot puff you up with pride if you understand the grace of God. People who are proud are really saying, "I am the reason things are working so well," and they look to themselves instead of to God. People who are living in the grace of God are always looking to Jesus. They are living with a sense of thankfulness, knowing that He's the One who has given them every good gift and every good thing that they have.

UNLIMITED GRACE TO CHANGE

Sometimes people confuse the grace of God with fatalism. Fatalism is the idea that we cannot change our circumstances despite what we do, so we just allow fate to take its course. Although we are totally dependent on the grace of God, it does not mean we sit passively and do nothing to utilize grace. Grace must be diligently desired and accepted.

Imagine yourself lying in the sunshine on a grassy hill on a warm summer's day. A huge rock begins to roll down the hill toward you. Fatalism says, "There's nothing I can do about it. Being crushed by this rock must be my destiny." The grace of God says, "I do not have to just lie here and be crushed by a rock. I will accept and utilize the strength God has given me, and I will get out of its way!" Of course, there are things in life that we cannot change, but we must realize that, if it wasn't for the grace of God, things could be much worse. Many undesirable things that happen in our lives can be avoided when we take God at His Word and trust His grace to give us the wisdom and strength to see things changed. God wants to give us more and more of His grace to live victoriously as Christians on this earth: "*He gives us more grace...*" (James 4:6). At every turn, God is on the lookout to offer grace to us!

As parents to four children who are now adults, again and again my wife LaVerne and I had to receive grace to train them properly and give them suitable advice at the right time as they were growing up. We look back now and are convinced that, as parents, we are totally dependent upon the grace of God.

Responding in the grace of God always brings more freedom, hope, refreshment, and peace so that we can move ahead with God. Paul the apostle told a church of new believers to continue on in the grace of God even when they had opposition:

Now when the congregation had broken up, many of the Jews and devout proselytes followed Paul and Barnabas, who, speaking to them, persuaded them to continue in the grace of God (Acts 13:43).

Paul knew that this recently established church of new believers had to have a clear understanding of grace in order to continue to move ahead in His purposes. Otherwise they would succumb to the tactics of the devil and forget that God's grace was sufficient.

277

FALLING SHORT OF GOD'S GRACE

Jesus told a parable one day about a landowner who had a vineyard (see Matt. 20:11-15). The grapes were ready to pick, so the landowner found some willing workers and sent them out at 9:00 A.M. to pick grapes. Later, he hired some more men and sent them out at 12:00 noon. Later still, he employed other workers and sent them out at 3:00 P.M. The grape crop was still not completely picked, so at 5:00 P.M., he sent some final laborers out to complete the harvest for the day. At the end of the day, he called all of the laborers in and gave them exactly the same amount of money because that is what he had promised each group at the start of their job. When the workers who toiled the longest hours discovered that the workers who labored only a few hours were paid the same, they complained to the landowner.

If this doesn't sound fair to you, you do not yet understand the grace of God. God loves us unconditionally, just the way we are. When we are secure in His love and acceptance, we no longer are concerned if someone else "gets a better deal" than we do. We live by grace, completely satisfied. When we understand that God's love and acceptance can't be earned or deserved, we live in the blessing of His grace each day.

Did you know that we will never be jealous and become bitter if we understand and live in the grace of God? Hebrews 12:15 says it like this: *"See to it that no one misses the grace of God and that no bitter root grows up to cause trouble and defile many."* Bitterness starts out like a small root. Did you ever see a sidewalk where roots had pushed up and cracked the concrete? It started with just one little root. Many times, people get bitter at God. They say, "God, why is that person prosperous, and I am struggling financially?" They have fallen short of the grace of God.

First Corinthians 10:12 says, *"So, if you think you are standing firm, be careful that you don't fall!"* If we are at the place where we think we are strong, and we're going to be OK, and we're not going to fall, the Bible says, "Be careful." Any of us can fall short of the grace of God in our lives.

GRACE TO THE HUMBLE

There is tremendous spiritual power released when we begin to experience the grace of God. Years ago, I was involved in a youth ministry. I remember coming home one day and discovering that someone had taken a big rock and thrown it through our window. I knew that the rock-thrower was someone we cared about and to whom we had ministered. God was teaching us about His grace, so the Lord helped us to take the attitude that it was only by His grace that our whole house did not have every window broken! We could have cried and complained, but God's grace gave us the power to move on so that we could continue to build His life in the people that He had placed in our lives. First Peter 5:5-6 says that *"God opposes the proud but gives grace to the humble. Humble your-selves, therefore, under God's mighty hand, that He may lift you up in due time."*

Humility is an attitude of total dependence on Jesus Christ. Pride is the opposite of a healthy understanding of the grace of God. The Scripture makes it clear that if we humble ourselves under the mighty hand of God, He will exalt us in due time. God wants to exalt you. He wants to honor you. When are we honored by God? When we humble ourselves before Him. If I try to do God's job, if I

279

try to exalt myself, then God would have to do my job. He would have to humble me. I would rather humble myself and allow God to exalt me than exalt myself and have God humble me—wouldn't you?

Humility places us in a position to receive this grace. True humility is constantly acknowledging that without Jesus we can do nothing but that with Jesus we can do all things. Humility isn't walking with your head bowed down, trying to look humble. True humility is understanding and living out the principle of the grace of God.

SEASON YOUR SPEECH WITH GRACE

We will not gossip if we understand the grace of God. The reason people gossip is because of false humility. Those who gossip try to elevate themselves on a pedestal as they look down on others. When someone is going through a difficult time or is involved in sin, we may be tempted to gossip about them. We will quickly stop gossiping when we remember that it is only by the grace of God that we are not going through the same things that they are experiencing.

The words that we speak are very powerful! Words are like dynamite. They can either be used powerfully for good, or they can be used powerfully for evil. Colossians 4:6 says,

Let your conversation be always full of grace, seasoned with salt, so that you may know how to answer everyone.

How can we speak with grace, seasoned with salt? When I was growing up, I never liked eating beef liver, but when I got married, I discovered that I had a beef-liver-eating wife! One day she served a beautiful meal. The meat smelled and tasted delicious. I said, "Honey, what is this? This meat is really good."

My wife, LaVerne, grinned from ear to ear. "It's liver!" She had seasoned it with the right kind of seasoning, and I liked it.

If you feel like you need to share correction with a struggling person that will help him or her to get back on the right course, season your speech with grace. In other words, say it in a way he or she can receive it. How we say it (with the right attitude) can be as important, if not more important, than what we actually say. Even a word of correction seasoned with grace will tell someone, "I care about you, and you can make it." The Bible tells us to speak the truth in love (see Eph. 4:15).

GOD'S GRACE THROUGH SUFFERING

Down through the ages, men and women have asked the question, "How can God be good and allow us to suffer?" I like the simple answer given by a Nazi concentration camp inmate: "When you know God, you don't need to know why."[1] The important issue is that God is involved in our sufferings. He came and entered our condition—became sin for us, so that we might become the righteousness of God (see 2 Cor. 5:21).

In fact, God tells us that we are to expect suffering (see John 16:33). There are many reasons why we suffer—sometimes it is a consequence of our own actions, of living in a sinful world, or of demonic affliction. If we allow Him to, God will use suffering as a catalyst to spiritual growth in our lives.

Being faithful to God does not guarantee that we will be free from trouble or pain in this life. Job, Joseph, David, Jeremiah—the list goes on—all suffered for a variety of reasons. Paul experienced many trials: he was put in chains, and experienced storms and shipwreck. Yet he still proclaimed that no tragedy could *"separate us from the love of God"* (see Rom. 8:35-39).

In addition, the Lord will not allow us to be tempted beyond what we can bear (see 1 Cor. 10:13). He will provide a way out so that we can stand up under our trials. Our suffering actually opens us up to Christ's abundant grace, according to Second Corinthians 12:9:

> *My grace is sufficient for you, for my power is made perfect in weakness....*

In our weakness or suffering, we can count on His strength to make us strong. In our times of tears, troubles, sickness, weaknesses, and fears, we can be strong because we have exchanged His strength for our weakness. Our strength comes from His strength, and His alone.

Often, during times of trials and struggles, we find that God's grace is very real to us. The Israelites found grace even in the desolate desert:

> *The people who survived the sword found grace in the wilderness...* (Jeremiah 31:2 NKJV).

Paul says in Romans 8:28 that *"in all things God works for the good of those who love Him."* If we continue to love and obey Him, He will give us the grace necessary to bear our affliction. The Bible says that Christians are like *"jars of clay"* who sometime experience sadness and pain, yet because of the heavenly treasure (Jesus) within, they are not defeated or crushed.

> *But we have this treasure in jars of clay to show that this all-surpassing power is from God and not from us. We are hard*

pressed on every side, but not crushed; perplexed, but not in despair (2 Corinthians 4:7-8).

In the midst of all of the sufferings and pressures of life, we are sustained by an inner life that cannot be defeated! I have found Jesus to be very close in my life during periods of greatest darkness. Jesus' abundant grace comes in troubled times.

ALLOW HIS GRACE TO MOTIVATE YOU

I used to grumble and think, "God, why do You allow me to experience bad days? I'm serving You. It just doesn't seem right." The Bible tells us, "*In everything give thanks, for this is the will of God in Christ Jesus concerning you*" (1 Thess. 5:18 NKJV). The Lord is teaching us to give thanks to Him in the midst of bad days. We need to count our blessings. By God's grace, we have so much for which to be thankful.

One day I was replacing a window in our home. I got frustrated, became careless, and broke the window. I realized then that I was trying to put the window in on my strength. I was frustrated and uptight and had moved out of the grace of God. When I admitted, "God, I cannot even put a window pane in without Your grace," do you know what happened? The next window went in with no problem. The grace of God affects even the practical day-to-day areas of our lives.

Some people love to go shopping. They may get a bargain and think, "This is great. It used to be $35, and I got it for $10! Man, wasn't I lucky?" Not really. It was the grace of God. The world system calls it luck. If you got a bargain while you were shopping, it was simply because of the grace of God on your life. The Lord wants us to thank and glorify Him for His grace to receive bargains. "Good luck" is the world system's replacement for the grace of God.

As a new Christian, I used to wonder why God would let my car break down so often. Now I realize that it was only by the grace of God that my old car did not completely quit years earlier! You may ask, "Does God want our cars to break down?" No, of course not, but God wants us, in every situation, to allow His grace to motivate us.

Paul firmly believed that, if we receive God's grace and later, by deliberate sin, abandon the faith, we can again be lost:

> As God's fellow workers we urge you not to receive God's grace in vain. For He says, 'In the time of My favor I heard you, and in the day of salvation I helped you.' I tell you, now is the time of God's favor, now is the day of salvation (2 Corinthians 6:1-2).

The grace of God affects us every day. We need to be sure never to take it for granted. As the comic strip character Pogo once stated, "We have met the enemy, and he is us." Only we can block the grace of God from flowing through our lives. If we find ourselves outside the grace of God, we are urged to be reconciled to God (see 2 Cor. 5:20). Now is the time to receive His grace and allow it to make a difference in our lives. Let's start today!

ENDNOTE

1. Grantley Morris, "No Loving God Would Let a Bystander Be Maimed by a Drunk Driver," *Arguments Against God and Christianity* (1996), www.geocities.com/heartland/estates/6535/ Questions/drunk.htm (accessed 15 Sept 2008).

RESPONDING TO GOD'S GRACE
REFLECTION QUESTIONS

1. Describe a time when you received grace to live victoriously.

2. What is a "root of bitterness," according to Hebrews 12:15? Does it ever cause trouble in your life?

3. Tell about a time when you spoke words "full of grace, seasoned with salt" into someone's life. What were the results?

4. How do suffering and grace work together, according to Second Corinthians 12:9?

Chapter 23

SPEAKING GRACE
to the MOUNTAIN

GRACE RELEASES DIVINE ENERGY

In the previous two chapters on grace, we described how God's grace is present in our lives to save us—"the free unmerited favor of God on the undeserving and ill-deserving." Let's focus now on another side of the "grace coin." The other side of God's grace is defined as "the power and desire to do God's will." The grace of God is literally "divine energy" that the Holy Spirit releases in our lives.

Here is a clear example from the Scriptures. Zerubbabel was faced with a formidable challenge (see Ezra 3). When Cyrus the king allowed the Jews to return to their own land, he appointed Zerubbabel to be the governor of the colony. One of Zerubbabel's first responsibilities was to lay the foundation for the new temple. However, due to opposition from the enemies of the Jews, the work on this project soon ceased.

Doesn't that sound familiar? We get a vision from the Lord or begin to take a direction in life, and before long we receive opposition, become discouraged, and quit. Or maybe we don't quit, but we seem to find it impossible to complete the task that we believe the Lord has laid before us. This is where grace comes in!

One day Zechariah the prophet was given a vision from the Lord. As he describes his vision in Zechariah 4:6-7, an angel of the Lord gives Zechariah a prophetic message for Zerubbabel:

> *"Not by might nor by power, but by my Spirit," says the Lord of Hosts. "Who are you, O great mountain? Before Zerubbabel you shall become a plain! And he shall bring forth the capstone with shouts of 'Grace, grace to it'"* (NKJV).

The work on the temple was resumed and completed four years later. The Lord gave them "divine energy," and the circumstances supernaturally changed for them to complete the entire project. That which seemed impossible literally happened before their very eyes. They no longer trusted in their own ability, but in the grace of God. As they released divine energy by shouting, "Grace, grace," the *mountain* before them became a *great plain*. They were convinced that the temple was built not by military might, or by political power or human strength, but by the Spirit of the Lord. They had experienced the grace of God!

We can only do God's work if we are enabled by the Holy Spirit. I dare you to apply this scriptural principle to your life. The next time a mountain of impossibility stares you in the face, shout "Grace, grace" to it. See the mountain leveled as you take an act of simple faith and shout "Grace, grace" in the face of the devil. You will find your focus changing from your ability (or lack of ability) to His ability.

Some time ago, I ministered to a group of university student leaders. We stood together and proclaimed, "Grace, grace" over every university campus represented at the conference. Faith arose in our hearts as our dependency was no longer in our own strategies and abilities but on the living God.

I find it refreshing to walk into our offices and hear staff persons declaring, "Grace, grace" in the midst of deadlines that seem impossible to meet. My faith is increased when fathers proclaim, "Grace, grace" over their families. Striving is replaced by a sense of peace and rest in the Lord.

When the children of Israel shouted, "Grace, grace" to the temple, they did not sit around and wait for the walls to be built by an angel. They had a renewed sense that, as they worked together, fulfilling the plan of God, it was not by their own might or power, but by the Spirit of the Lord that the walls were being built. As we proclaim, "Grace, grace" over our lives and situations, we do not receive a license to be lazy. Instead, we receive divine energy to fulfill the purposes of God for our lives.

SPEAK GRACE TO IMPOSSIBLE SITUATIONS

Skeptics may say, "What does shouting 'Grace, grace' have to do with God acting on our behalf? It seems so foolish." The truth is that the wisdom of God and the wisdom of the world are at odds:

For the message of the cross is foolishness to those who are perishing, but to us who are being saved it is the power of God (1 Corinthians 1:18).

The wisdom of the world is a wisdom that excludes God and emphasizes our ability to take care of things ourselves. God's wisdom emphasizes a complete dependency on God and His grace. God honors this dependency and obedience to Him.

Why did the army advance only when Moses held up his arms in the battle with the Amalekites? It made absolutely no sense to the natural mind, but Moses was being obedient to his God (see Exod. 17).

Jehoash, the king of Israel, came to Elisha, the prophet, for help because the Israelite army faced a massive Aramean army. It seemed like an impossible situation. Elisha instructed King Jehoash to take a bow and some arrows and open the east window. Then Elisha told him to shoot and declared that they would have victory. In addition, the prophet told Jehoash to "strike the ground." The king struck the ground three times and stopped. The prophet Elisha was angry with the king: *"You should have struck the ground five or six times; then you would have defeated Aram and completely destroyed it. But now you will defeat it only three times"* (2 Kings 13:19). It happened just as the prophet said. King Jehoash showed that he lacked the commitment and faith necessary for the Lord to fulfill His promise. Consequently, he could not completely defeat the Arameans.

What does striking the ground with arrows have to do with winning battles? Nothing, unless the Lord instructs us to do it. In the same way that Elisha instructed King Jehoash to strike the ground with arrows, I believe the Lord is calling His people to be obedient and shout "Grace, grace" to situations that seem impossible to them.

GRACE TO REIGN IN LIFE

A king reigns in a nation, and as God's children, we are promised to reign in life. How do we reign? We can reign, or be victorious, only by His grace. We receive grace to reign in life: *"...those who receive God's abundant provision of grace and of the gift of righteousness reign in life through the one man, Jesus Christ"* (Rom. 5:17).

This promise is for all of us. Those who receive God's overflowing grace and the free gift of righteousness will reign as kings in life. We are called to live above the circumstances, difficulties, and problems because reigning comes from understanding the grace of God.

We can be victorious in every area of life—in our homes, in school, in our small groups and churches, and in our places of business. God has given us supernatural provision to live an overcomer's life. God gives us an abundance of grace. We do not deserve any of it, but the Lord pours it on us anyway.

Are you struggling with a habit that you have tried to break free from? Speak "Grace, grace" to it! Receive the divine energy that is needed to break free forever. Are you struggling in business, school, or family relationships? Speak "Grace, grace" to the area of your life that seems like an impossible mountain to cross.

I had the privilege of addressing the students of Lifeway School in New Zealand where a proposed building project had come to a halt due to a lack of finances. Along with the students and the leadership of the school, we positioned ourselves toward the plot of land that was undeveloped and shouted, "Grace, grace." Within the next eight weeks, the school experienced a series of financial miracles, and the expansion of the facilities got underway. The only explanation was the grace of God.

There are times when I'm speaking or counseling someone, and after I leave, I'll feel discouraged. Satan often tries to place condemnation on us so that he can defeat us by capitalizing on the way we feel or the blunders we made. We must live by faith, not by our feelings. When things go bad, whether in our business, school, community, home, or church, we must never forget that God's grace gives us divine energy to push on through. When things are fine, we must not forget that it is only by God's grace that we are experiencing victory to reign in life.

GIFTS ACCORDING TO GRACE

God's grace is so rich and multifaceted that a different aspect of it can be manifested through every believer. God gives gifts, inward motivations, and abilities to believers so that they may use them to benefit the rest of the Body of Christ. These "grace gifts" are given to enable us to minister to others:

Having then gifts differing according to the grace that is given to us, let us use them... (Romans 12:6a NKJV)

...If a man's gift is prophesying, let him use it in proportion to his faith. If it is serving, let him serve; if it is teaching, let him teach; if it is encouraging, let him encourage; if it is contributing to the needs of others, let him give generously; if it is leadership, let him govern diligently; if it is showing mercy, let him do it cheerfully (Romans 12:6b-8).

Have you ever shared your faith with somebody and sensed the Holy Spirit moving through you as the right words came flowing from your mouth? This was simply the grace of God on your life as you shared the Gospel. Do you enjoy serving? God has given you the desire and ability to give practical assistance to others. Teaching is the ability to examine God's Word and proclaim its truth so that people grow in godliness. We should use the gifts to go about fulfilling God's purposes for our lives according to what He has given us. Each gift and ability that we have is a result of God's grace. He has given us these gifts and blessings in order to be a blessing and to serve others:

Each one should use whatever gift he has received to serve others, faithfully administering God's grace in its various forms (1 Peter 4:10).

The gifts that the Lord gives to us are divine abilities that we use to help and bless others. If you have the gift of prophecy, use it to speak encouragement and conviction in someone's life. If you have an inward motivation to give, those around you will be blessed by your financial help. When you operate in your gift(s), you are being used of the Lord to express His grace to others.

COMPARING IS NOT WISE

Remember the grape-picking laborers in Matthew 20? They complained and wondered why everyone got paid the same for varying hours of labor because they didn't understand the grace of God. If we question why God gives some people greater talents and abilities than others, we have not understood the grace of God. If we think that we are a better worship leader than Jim or a better teacher than Sally, we are falling short of God's grace.

It is so important to refrain from comparing ourselves with others. We should only compare ourselves with the Word of God and allow the Word to dwell in us so that we can live out the principles of grace in our lives. If we feel like we are doing better than others, we fall into pride. If we feel like we are doing worse than those around us, we can suffer from feelings of inferiority. When we compare ourselves to others, we are not wise, according to God's Word in Second Corinthians 10:12: "*We do not dare to classify or compare ourselves with some who commend themselves. When they measure themselves by themselves and compare themselves with themselves, they are not wise."* Neither pride nor inferiority are grace-filled responses.

When God uses someone else for a certain ministry or responsibility, and we are not called into action, how do we respond? When we begin to compare ourselves to other people, we are falling short of the grace of God. God is God. He knows best what we need. He may give somebody one gift and somebody else a different type of gift. Understanding and walking in the grace of God will permeate our total being and way of thinking. It changes our attitudes, causing us to want to grow up spiritually so that we can help and serve those around us.

IMPART GRACE TO OTHERS

God has called you to impart His grace everywhere that you go—work, school, home, or to other believers in your small group. He has called you to impart grace to people and to see them built up:

> *Do not let any unwholesome talk come out of your mouths, but only what is helpful for building others up according to their needs, that it may benefit those who listen* (Ephesians 4:29).

When we speak, we should say things that build people up so that we can impart grace (divine energy) into their lives. Words of encouragement will minister to others the grace that God has placed in our lives. When you thank your spouse, your parents, or another family member, you are ministering the grace of God to them. Thank your boss for his oversight at work. You are ministering the grace of God. Maybe you are a boss. You need to give encouragement to the people who work for you. You are ministering the grace of God to them.

Why not encourage your small group leader and minister grace to him or her? Encourage your leaders and thank them for what they have done. The grace of God should be the underlying attitude in everything that we do. The Book of Acts tells us that "much grace" was on the apostles:

With great power the apostles continued to testify to the resurrection of the Lord Jesus, and much grace was upon them all (Acts 4:33).

We need a dose of God's "much grace" each day. John, the apostle, tells us that grace and truth come through Jesus Christ (see John 1:17). Jesus has already granted us grace for our salvation. He is waiting for us to acknowledge Him and His grace so that we can experience His divine energy in our everyday living!

We should be careful not to allow discouraging words to come out of our mouths. Think of some people to whom the Lord may be asking you to minister His grace today, and do it!

ALL CREDIT GOES TO GOD

We will never take credit for what God does if we understand His grace. For example, I have had the privilege of ministering to many people throughout the world in the past few years. It has been such a blessing to see people's lives changed by the power of God. I could never take credit for that. I know that it is only by the grace of God that I can minister the good news of Jesus Christ.

The Bible tells us that we are all competent ministers (see 2 Cor. 3:5); we are called to help other people and to minister in Jesus' name. We are not ministering to others in our own strength, but God who lives inside of us is ministering through us. You and I are called to be channels of God's love.

Electric wire is a channel for electric power. We don't see an electric line and think, "What a beautiful wire." No, we are just thankful for the power that comes through the wire. Likewise, we are channels of the Holy Spirit, and we can never take credit for anything that God does. We must allow His grace and power to flow from our lives. We have been chosen as heirs of Christ to carry His banner, *"having been justified by His grace"* (Titus 3:7). What an awesome privilege—of all the people in the world, He has chosen you and me!

I encourage you to begin to shout "Grace, grace" to the mountains in your life. Remember Zerubbabel? He knew that the grace of God would be released and that the people would get the job completed quickly, effectively, and efficiently if he was obedient. So the people shouted, "Grace, grace" to the temple, and it was completed, causing great excitement among the people. They realized that it wasn't their strength but the strength of God's grace working through them.

No matter what situation you find yourself in, you need to learn to speak "Grace, grace" to it. If you have a habit that you want to conquer, but you have repeatedly fallen flat on your face, begin to speak "grace" to that situation. Maybe you are a businessman and struggling financially. Begin to speak grace to your business. Perhaps you are encouraging a new believer who is dealing with some area of his or her life. Begin to speak grace to that area. Is there a conflict in your marriage? Maybe you are a single person and have a special need. Begin to speak grace to your life. Maybe your prayer life needs revitalizing. Speak grace to your prayer life.

The commander in chief of the armies of heaven is waiting for us to declare "Grace, grace" over our families, our churches, our cities, and our nations. *"The kingdoms of this world have become the kingdoms of our Lord and of His Christ, and He shall reign forever and ever!"* (Rev. 11:15 NKJV).

"Grace, grace!"

Speaking Grace to the Mountain
Reflection Questions

1. Explain "divine energy." How is it at work in your life?

2. According to Romans 5:17, how do we get the power to reign as kings in this life? List struggles that you are having, and shout "grace" to them. What do you expect to happen?

3. Describe a time when you imparted grace into someone's life. Did you see immediate results or not?

4. List areas of your life that need grace applied to them.

Chapter 24

GRACE FOR EVERYDAY LIVING

GROW IN GRACE

When I was young in the Lord, I did not understand grace at all. I thought that God really owed me something. "Look, God," I said, "I've given you my life. I've given you everything. I've given you my family. It all belongs to you." I was working 60 hours on a job in addition to being involved with a full-time youth ministry. I thought, "God, you have to take care of my family. You have to take care of my relationship with my wife. After all, I'm serving you; I'm giving you my life." I later realized that God didn't owe me anything. God did not owe me a strong marriage or a healthy family. But even though I did not deserve it, God wanted to give me a strong marriage and family because of His awesome grace. Praise God for His grace!

The grace of God will affect every area of your life. We can do absolutely nothing except by the grace of God. Do we deserve a bright, sunny, summer day? No. But we receive the sunshine because of the grace of God. We stand in a position for the sun to shine on us, and when we see the sun, we receive it. As Christians, we need to get into a position to receive the grace of God in our lives. However, growing in grace is a process. It doesn't just happen overnight: "*But*

299

grow in the grace and knowledge of our Lord and Savior Jesus Christ. To Him be glory both now and forever. Amen" (2 Pet. 3:18).

God gives us grace to grow every step of the way if we walk in obedience to Him. We were saved because of God's grace through faith (see Eph. 2:5,8), and we continue to receive grace to live the Christian life. In this chapter, we will look at several areas in our daily lives that God wants to invade and keep permeating with His grace.

THE FRUIT OF THE SPIRIT

How, then, do we grow in grace? The Spirit and our sinful nature are at war with each other. Since the sinful nature remains within us after our conversion and is our deadly enemy (see Rom. 8:6-8,13; Gal. 5:17,21), it must be resisted and put to death in a continual warfare that we wage through the power of the Holy Spirit (see Rom. 8:4-14). If we do not fight a battle against our sinful nature but continue to practice the acts of the sinful nature, the Bible says that we cannot inherit God's Kingdom (see Gal. 5:21). According to Galatians 5:19-21, our sinful nature causes us to fall into such terrible things as sexual immorality, impurity, debauchery, idolatry, witchcraft, hatred, discord, jealousy, fits of rage, selfish ambition, dissensions, factions, envy, drunkenness, and orgies.

Thank God for His grace because this passage in Galatians goes on to say that when we fellowship with God, He produces the fruit of the Spirit in our lives:

> *But the fruit of the Spirit is love, joy, peace, patience, kindness, goodness, faithfulness, gentleness and self-control.... Those who belong to Christ Jesus have crucified the sinful*

nature with its passions and desires. Since we live by the Spirit, let us keep in step with the Spirit. (Galatians 5:22-26).

The contrast between the lifestyle of the Spirit-filled Christian and one who is controlled by his sinful nature is clear. Our human nature with its corrupt desires is our "sinful nature." When we depend on God's grace to live a lifestyle of love, joy, peace, patience, kindness, goodness, faithfulness, gentleness, and self-control, we will experience these virtues or "fruits" in our lives. When we allow the Holy Spirit to direct our lives, sin's power is destroyed. We can then walk in fellowship with God, and by His grace, He will produce the fruit of the Spirit to help us live victoriously in every area of our lives.[1]

GRACE TO LIVE SEXUALLY PURE

Standards for sexual morality are clear in God's Word. Believers must live morally and sexually pure lives, according to Hebrews 13:4:

Marriage should be honored by all, and the marriage bed kept pure, for God will judge the adulterer and all the sexually immoral.

The word *pure* in the Greek means "to be free from corrupt desire."[2] It suggests refraining from all acts and thoughts that incite desire not in accordance with one's virginity or one's marriage vows. It stresses restraint and avoidance of all sexual actions and excitements that would defile our purity before God. It includes controlling our own bodies *"in a way that is holy and honorable,"* and not in *"passionate lust"* (1 Thess. 4:4-5). This scriptural instruction is for both those who are single and those who are married.[3]

Sexual intimacy has boundaries. It is reserved for the marriage relationship, in which a man and a woman become one. In that arena, God blesses the relationship with the physical and emotional pleasures that result.

Premarital sex is condemned in the Bible. The Bible says, "...*The body is not meant for sexual immorality, but for the Lord, and the Lord for the body*" (1 Cor. 6:13). Verse 18 goes on to say, "*Flee from sexual immorality. All other sins a man commits are outside his body, but he who sins sexually sins against his own body.*" Galatians 5:19 says, "*The acts of the sinful nature are obvious: sexual immorality, impurity...*" Ephesians 5:3 says it most plainly, "*But among you there must not be even a hint of sexual immorality, or of any kind of impurity, or of greed, because these are improper for God's holy people.*" From these verses, we see that the Bible promotes complete and total abstinence from premarital sex. Virginity until marriage is God's sexual standard of purity for men and women.

What about homosexuality? Homosexual or gay and lesbian persons have often been excluded and persecuted by a culture that hypocritically glorifies other forms of sexual sin. A gay person should not be treated differently from those who have fallen victim to other types of sin. Homosexual practice is sin (see Rom. 1:26-27; 1 Tim. 1:9-10), but sin is by no means unique to homosexuals. We are all sinners. In First Corinthians 6:9-11, Paul describes homosexuality as a sin, but he calls upon Christians to treat the homosexual as a person who is in need of forgiveness and transformation:

Do you not know that the wicked will not inherit the kingdom of God? Do not be deceived: Neither the sexually immoral nor idolaters nor adulterers nor male prostitutes nor

> *homosexual offenders nor thieves nor the greedy nor drunk-
> ards nor slanderers nor swindlers will inherit the kingdom of
> God. And that is what some of you were. But you were
> washed, you were sanctified, you were justified in the name
> of the Lord Jesus Christ and by the Spirit of our God.*

Sometimes Christians continue to struggle with same-sex attrac-
tion. Understanding and wise guidance can make the difference in
helping those attracted to the same sex to avoid homosexual activity altogether. Both those who are tempted and those who are
already caught in sin (see Gal. 6:1) need to be restored in a spirit of
compassion and gentleness. As Christians, we must be ministers of
God's transforming grace toward homosexuals and those struggling
with temptations. The Bible provides hope for every sinner.
Everyone is equally in need of God's grace. We must love people as
we point them toward the victorious life that is possible through
Jesus Christ.

GRACE FOR MARRIAGE

Marriage is God's idea. Genesis 2:24 implies that marriage is an
exclusive relationship (*a man...his wife*), which is publicly acknowledged (*leaves his parents*), permanent (*cleaves to his wife*), and con-
summated by having sexual relations (*they will become one flesh*).
The marriage bond is a divine covenant that is intended to last for
life. Fidelity, support, and mutual sharing as the husband and wife
build the life of Christ in each other are at the center of the relationship.

God gave Adam and Eve rulership over every living creature (see
Gen. 1:28). He then placed them in the Garden of Eden to care for
His creation (see Gen. 2:15). He created order so that things would

not be in chaos in the world. The same is true of marriage. The scriptural basis for order in Christian marriage is found in Ephesians 5:21-33:

> *Submit to one another out of reverence for Christ. Wives, submit to your husbands as to the Lord. For the husband is the head of the wife as Christ is the head of the church, His body, of which He is the Savior....In this same way, husbands ought to love their wives as their own bodies. He who loves his wife loves himself. After all, no one ever hated his own body, but he feeds and cares for it, just as Christ does the church—for we are members of His body. "For this reason a man will leave his father and mother and be united to his wife, and the two will become one flesh." This is a profound mystery—but I am talking about Christ and the church. However, each one of you also must love his wife as he loves himself, and the wife must respect her husband.*

Husbands and wives need to submit to each other in love. This Scripture says that the husband is positionally the "head" of the wife, which means that he is the responsible one. Responsibility, however, does not mean control. In today's world, where domestic violence is a huge problem, we can never think that physical or verbal abuse is about a lack of submission. Selfishness and control is not a form of headship. Any kind of abuse in marriage, including physical, emotional, spiritual, or sexual abuse, is wrong. If physical abuse occurs, a spouse should seek a safe place.

Marriage is instituted by God so that men and women can mutually complete each other. Marriage takes two people working hard at nourishing this bond. Sadly, in today's world, the incidence of divorce has reached epidemic proportions. What about a marriage that has failed? Read the next section for some answers.

GRACE WHEN A MARRIAGE FAILS

Reconciliation lies at the very heart of Christianity. Although Scripture cites two biblical grounds for divorce, every effort should be made to restore a marriage. Paul the apostle wrote to the Corinthian church,

> *Are you married? Do not seek a divorce...* (1 Corinthians 7:27a).

When the Pharisees asked Jesus about the grounds for divorce, He referred them to the original institution of marriage (see Matt. 19:3-8), stressing that marriage is intended for life. God hates divorce (see Mal. 2:13-16). Divorce is devastating. It has an effect, not just on two people, but on their children and families. Reconciliation in marriage is God's desire (see 1 Cor. 7:12-14). However, sometimes reconciliation is not possible. In this case, God's Word cites two reasons when divorce is permitted—for marital unfaithfulness (see Matt. 5:31-32; 19:9) or for abandonment (see 1 Cor. 7:15-16).

Failure in marriage often has *selfishness* as its roots. We want what we want! Regardless of the reasons, we have to face the facts: today's world is full of broken marriages. We must minister with compassion to those facing a failed marriage.

Those going through a divorce have experienced a breakdown in trust. At this crucial and heartbreaking time, a person going through a divorce needs prayerful accountability with trusted church leadership or counselors. They will need to deal with trust and fear issues (How can I ever trust a spouse again? What will keep another marriage from failing?).

Some of the most heroic people are those who have been sinned against by having to experience abandonment, separation, and/or divorce unwillingly. These persons have not sinned, but they feel rejected by many in the Church today. Jesus does not abandon, separate from (reject), or divorce those who are His. During these times, His grace will increase!

> *Marriage should be honored by all, and the marriage bed kept pure, for God will judge the adulterer and all the sexually immoral…God has said, "Never will I leave you; never will I forsake you." So we say with confidence, "The Lord is my helper; I will not be afraid. What can man do to me?"* (Hebrews 13:4-6).

GRACE FOR SINGLES

We said earlier that sex is for marriage only. What does the Bible say about singleness? The world may say that a human cannot live without sexual experience, but the Bible disagrees. A single person can be fulfilled and live without sexual experience. Jesus referred to singleness as a divine vocation in Matthew 19:12:

> *Others have renounced marriage because of the kingdom of heaven. The one who can accept this should accept it.*

The apostle Paul said that one of the blessings of singleness is that it releases people to give their undivided devotion to Jesus.

> *I would like you to be free from concern. An unmarried man is concerned about the Lord's affairs—how he can please the Lord. But a married man is concerned about the affairs of this world—how he can please his wife—and his interests are divided. An unmarried woman or virgin is concerned about*

306

the Lord's affairs: Her aim is to be devoted to the Lord in both body and spirit. But a married woman is concerned about the affairs of this world—how she can please her husband. I am saying this for your own good, not to restrict you, but that you may live in a right way in undivided devotion to the Lord (1 Corinthians 7:32-35).

He also says that both singleness and marriage are a gift of God's grace: *"I wish that all men were as I am. But each man has his own gift from God; one has this gift, another has that"* (see 1 Cor. 7:7). Both the married person and unmarried will receive grace for the state in which they find themselves.

Unmarried people may be quite lonely at times, but God always gives the grace to live in obedience to Him. If you're single, you are not half of a person. You are whole in Christ. He wants you to be fulfilled as a single person, and He will give you the grace.

I have many friends who are single, and they are living a very abundant life. They have received grace from God to be fulfilled in their singleness. They have extra time available to minister to youth and to other singles. They have kept their eyes on Jesus and on His grace, and their lives are living proof of our God's faithfulness.

DON'T MISS GRACE

The writer of Hebrews 12:15 warns believers that they should not miss God's grace: *"See to it that no one misses the grace of God...."* We can miss God's grace when we try to live the Christian life by our own efforts. In Galatians 5:3-4, Paul says that the Galatians had moved from a faith in Christ to legalistic observances of the law. Thus, they had *"...fallen away from grace"* (Gal. 5:4).

Sometimes people say of someone who hurt them, "He really hurt my feelings." If we allow our hurt feelings to control our lives, we are not living in the realm of God's grace. Who says everyone should be nice to us? If we are misunderstood, the only reason it is not much worse is because of the grace of God. If we are hurt, we are demanding our own rights. But we do not have rights. They were nailed to the cross two thousand years ago. We no longer have a *right* not to get hurt. However, we do have *privileges* whereby we can live for God and experience a victorious life. These privileges that we have are the result of the grace of God.

Let it be clear that, as Christians, we do have rights against the devil. The Bible teaches us that we have spiritual rights as we stand against the devil to rebuke him in the name of Jesus. We have the right to use the name of Jesus, the blood of Christ, and the Word of God. But we need to realize that even that right is available because of the grace of God.

Often when I meet parents who have raised godly families, I ask them, "How did you do it?" I have not been surprised by their answer. They tell me that it was simply the grace of God. If we think that we deserve godly children, a good job, and good friends because we have done all the right things, we are simply wrong!

I am thankful that God has given me a wonderful family and marriage. But it is not because of anything that I have done. I am simply a recipient of the grace of God that I have received from Him as a free gift.

From start to finish, we must live our lives in God's grace. God's grace through faith brings salvation to us at the start of our Christian lives and continues giving us the power and ability to respond to God and resist sin. Grace is a wonderful gift that God gives because He loves us!

This concludes the first book in this two-book Biblical Foundation Series. In this book, we've learned the foundations of the Christian life and how to build our relationship with God. In the second book in this series, entitled *Building Your Life on the Basic Truths of Christianity*, we will learn more about deepening our relationship with God, but also about the importance of relating to others in the Church as we learn to serve others, handle money, reach out to those around us, and find our destiny.

ENDNOTES

1. For more about the fruit of the Spirit, read Larry Kreider and Sam Smucker, *Exercise the Fruit of the Spirit and Get Fit for Life*, (Lititz, PA: House to House Publications, 2008).

2. *The New Testament Greek Lexicon*, s.v. "Katharos" (pure), www.studylight.org/lex/grk/view.cgi?number=2513 (accessed 27 Sept 2008).

3. *Full Life Study Bible* (Grand Rapids, MI: Zondervan Publishing House, 1992), 1936.

GRACE FOR EVERYDAY LIVING
REFLECTION QUESTIONS

1. Tell of ways that you have grown in the grace of God.

2. Why is it important to live a sexually pure life (see Heb. 13:4)?

3. How can we minister with compassion to a person going through a divorce? Who will never leave us, according to Hebrews 13:4-6?

4. Explain the difference between having rights and privileges.

ADDITIONAL RESOURCES

WWW.DCFI.ORG

BUILDING YOUR PERSONAL HOUSE OF PRAYER

If you love to pray, or you need to pray more effectively, this book will change your prayer life forever. Your entire approach to prayer is about to improve! By Larry Kreider, 254 pages: $15.99 ISBN: 978-0-7684-2662-5

HEARING GOD 30 DIFFERENT WAYS

The Lord speaks to us in ways we often miss, including through the Bible, prayer, circumstances, spiritual gifts, conviction, His character, His peace, and even in times of silence. Take 30 days and discover how God's voice can become familiar to you as you develop a loving relationship with Him. By Larry Kreider, 224 pages: $14.99 ISBN: 978-1-886973-76-3

AUTHENTIC SPIRITUAL MENTORING

There is a desperate need for spiritually mature men and women to mentor younger believers to be fully equipped and faithful servants of Christ. Whether you are looking for a spiritual mentor or desiring to become one, this book is for you! By Larry Kreider, 224 pages: ISBN: 978-0-8307-4413-8

SPEAK LORD! I'M LISTENING

Jesus said, "My sheep hear my voice," but many Christians do not know how to hear from God. In this practical, story-rich guidebook, international teacher Larry Kreider shows believers how to develop a listening relationship with the Lord. It explores the multiple ways Christians can hear the voice of God in today's world, offering real-life examples—not theory—of how God teaches His followers to listen, with tips in each chapter for distinguishing His voice from the noise of satan's interference. Christians across the denominational spectrum will develop a closer and deeper relationship with God as they learn 50 unique ways to listen to Him. You will realize that God was speaking to you all along but, like the disciples on the road to Emmaus, you didn't know it was Him! By Larry Kreider, 224 pages: ISBN: 978-0-830746-12-5

EXERCISE THE FRUIT OF THE SPIRIT AND GET FIT FOR LIFE

This book encourages you to take a spiritual health check of your life to see if you are producing the Bible's nine exercises for spiritual wellness as mentioned in Galatians 5:22-23 and expressed in the believer as growing the fruit of the Spirit. By Larry Kreider and Sam Smucker, ISBN: 978-1-886973-93-0

THE BIBLICAL ROLE OF ELDERS FOR TODAY'S CHURCH

New Testament principles for equipping church leadership teams: Why leadership is needed, what their qualifications and responsibilities are, how they should be chosen, how elders function as spiritual fathers and mothers, how they are to make decisions, resolve conflicts, and more. By Larry Kreider, Ron Myer, Steve Prokopchak, and Brian Sauder, 274 pages: ISBN: 978-1-886973-62-6

HELPING YOU BUILD CELL CHURCHES MANUAL

A complete biblical blueprint for small groups, this manual covers 51 topics! Includes study and discussion questions. Use for training small group leaders or personal study. Compiled by Brian Sauder and Larry Kreider, 224 pages: ISBN: 978-1-886973-38-1

CHURCH PLANTING AND LEADERSHIP TRAINING

(LIVE OR VIDEO SCHOOL WITH LARRY KREIDER AND OTHERS)

Prepare now for a lifetime of ministry and service to others. The purpose of this school is to train the leaders our world is desperately looking for. We provide practical information as well as Holy Spirit empowered impartation and activation. Be transformed and prepared for a lifetime of ministry and service to others.

If you know where you are called to serve...church, small group, business, public service, marketplace, or if you simply want to grow in your leadership ability—our goal is to help you build a biblical foundation to be led by the Holy Spirit and pursue your God-given dreams. **For a complete list of classes and venues, visit www.dcfi.org.**

SCHOOL OF GLOBAL TRANSFORMATION (SEVEN-MONTH RESIDENTIAL DISCIPLESHIP SCHOOL)

Be equipped for a lifetime of service in the church, marketplace and beyond! The School of Global Transformation is a seven-month residential discipleship school that runs September through March. Take seven months to satisfy your hunger for more of God. Experience His love in a deeper way than you ever dreamed possible. He has a distinctive plan and purpose for your life. We are committed to helping students discover destiny in Him and prepare them to transform the world around them.

For details visit www.dcfi.org.

SEMINARS

One-day **Seminars** with Larry Kreider and other DOVE Christian Fellowship International authors and leaders:

Building a Biblical Foundation for Your Life

Building Your Personal House of Prayer

How to Fulfill Your Calling as a Spiritual Father/Mother

How to Build Healthy Leadership Teams

How to Hear God—30 Different Ways

Called Together Couple Mentoring

How to Build Small Groups—Basics

How to Grow Small Groups—Advanced

Counseling Basics

Effective Fivefold Ministry Made Practical

Starting House Churches

Planting Churches Made Practical

How to Live in Kingdom Prosperity

How to Equip and Release Prophetic Ministry

FOR MORE INFORMATION ABOUT DCFI SEMINARS,
CALL 800-848-5892.

E-MAIL: SEMINARS@DCFI.ORG

CONTACT INFORMATION FOR SPEAKING ENGAGEMENTS:

Larry Kreider, International Director

DOVE Christian Fellowship International

11 Toll Gate Road

Lititz, PA 17543

Website: www.dcfi.org

E-mail:LarryK@dcfi.org

Additional copies of this book and other book titles from DESTINY IMAGE are available at your local bookstore.

Call toll-free: 1-800-722-6774.

Send a request for a catalog to:

Destiny Image® Publishers, Inc.
P.O. Box 310
Shippensburg, PA 17257-0310

"Speaking to the Purposes of God for This Generation and for the Generations to Come."

For a complete list of our titles, visit us at www.destinyimage.com.